"Verily, verily, I say unto you, that when I give a commandment to any of the sons of men to do a work unto my name, and those sons of men go with all their might and with all they have to perform that work, and cease not their diligence, and their enemies come upon them and hinder them from performing that work, behold, it behooveth me to require that work no more at the hands of those sons of men, but to accept of their offerings."
(Doctrine and Covenants 124:49)

Home Early
... Now What?

How to Navigate Coming Home Early from a Mission

Destiny Yarbro

(and Many Other Early-Returned Missionaries)

I know this is a confusing time! Truly, I hope this book will help you navigate this trial. You're in my prayers.

Destiny Yarbro

The Story Behind the Cover Photo

Elder Wesley Wright was sent home due to unworthiness prior to the mission. This photo was taken when his mission president welcomed him back to the mission with open arms after six months at home.

"I've never once excused myself or created a lie as to why I've returned home, to anyone that has ever asked me. In my eyes, doing such would only prevent others from seeing and feeling how grateful I am that I can be forgiven because of my Savior Jesus Christ. I love my Heavenly Father, and I love my Savior, who has given me this second chance."

While this photo may not represent every early RM's experience, Elder Wright's mom said it perfectly: "This is how I envision our Heavenly Father welcoming us home after we have tried to overcome our shortcomings."

The cover photograph is used with permission by Emily Palmer.

Cover design by Shayna Collier Nelson.

This book is dedicated to

The Hungarian Saints Who Are Ever in My Heart

My Companions Who Stuck by Me

My Eternal Family Who Loves Me

My Heavenly Father Who Never Gave Up on Me

and the myriad of others who helped make this book happen
over the last three and a half years.

First Printing, Nov 2017
ISBN 978-1537719597
1109 N Temple Dr
Provo, UT 84604
www.earlyRM.com

CONTENTS

—

BEFORE WE BEGIN

—

> "It's one of my theories that when people give
> you advice, they're really just talking to
> themselves in the past."
> *Austin Kleon*

Hello Friend!

It's great to see that either you have found this little book online or someone who cares about you has given it to you as a gift. I look forward to helping you navigate this journey!

Before we get started I need to make a few things clear. (Parents, mission presidents, bishops, ward members, and anyone else who happens to be reading this may want to pay attention as well.)

WHAT THIS BOOK ISN'T

This book is not simply an autobiography of one early-returned missionary ... aka ME. That would be kind of dull, wouldn't it? This is a compilation of thoughts, stories, challenges, encouragements, frustrations, ideas, and understandings from many early-returned missionaries. I just happen to be the narrator.

This book is not a happy-go-lucky guide that says coming home is as easy as pie. It is definitely written by actual early-returned missionaries who understand a lot about what coming home early entails. At the same time, this is not a book where disgruntled returned missionaries get together to vent or bag on the Church. Don't worry, this book encourages faith in and turning to our Father in Heaven for support!

This book is not written solely for missionaries who came home with a medical release. Missionaries who came home for broken legs, depression, trauma, transgression, a death in the family, and a myriad of other reasons are all represented. It's tricky to write a book addressing all of these individual circumstances, but I hope that you will relate to at least one story from a missionary. Keep your eyes peeled for anything that applies to *you*!

This book is not an official Church publication.
While it is written to build faith and hope in alignment with gospel principles, this contains the opinions and suggestions of many early RMs and is not an official publication of the Church. On nearly every other page, however, there are quotes from Church leaders, LDS authors, and other inspired materials.

WHAT THIS BOOK IS

This book will help you recognize that:

1. You are not alone! There are quite a few of us who have come home early.
2. It *is* possible to come home early and stay active in the Church!

3. Coming home earlier than expected is not the end of your spiritual journey, no matter what the reason for your return!

4. While many may not understand your situation or circumstances, you can proactively help them support your faithful efforts to stay strong! (Ideas on how to work with family, ward members, and priesthood leaders will be provided later in this book.)

5. Most importantly, turn to the Lord during this trial and you will be okay in time. Remember, "all things work together for good to them that love God" (Romans 8:28).

This book is a basic guide for any early-returned missionary. *Basic* is the key word. I'm not a pro at coming home early. In fact, there are *many* things I wish I would have done better. But the reason I feel confident in recommending this book to you is that a large number of the pages are written by early-returned missionaries other than me! :)

This book is not perfect. Many of you may find that only 50% of the material inside applies to you. Or you may feel that the title "early-returned missionaries" is not the right name for us. For convenience, I will use "early RM" from here on out to represent missionaries who came home earlier than anticipated. While it is certainly not my intention to offend anyone, I understand that this may happen. Please know any offense given is unintentional. Please pray to feel the spirit of this book—all the many writers and I truly want to help you on your journey and not offend you in any way!

This book is for all early-returned missionaries. It doesn't matter if you came home today or if you returned 20 years ago, whether you are currently active or inactive in the Church, I just hope that you will find something in here that helps you in your journey. While some of the wording will be directed to more recently returned missionaries, many of the early-returned missionaries who helped me write this book came home many years ago.

This is the book I wish I would have had when I came home. From what I can tell, this is the first book of its kind. Every time I had writer's block, I thought about what I wish I could have read when I first walked off the plane in 2009. I sure hope this can be a reference guide for you about that time when you don't quite know what to do...and it'll certainly be a future reference for me too!

Two Last Things I Have to Say...

YOU CAN DO THIS!!! Coming home probably feels overwhelming. It certainly was for me when I came home. There are so many unanswered questions, unique challenges, and misunderstandings around you. Just remember to hang in there, friend!

GO AT YOUR OWN PACE. Don't feel like you need to read every page today, tomorrow, or even this week. Your journey will take a while, and you can read through this book slowly or skip around to chapters that apply most to you today. Sadly, not every page will be pleasant; this book will help you heal, which is rarely a very pleasant experience. Give yourself a break sometimes. Let yourself have a lousy day. Take a breath every once in a while. After a day or so, come back and read some more so that you can make the next step in your progress.

And Now, Let's Begin!

Okay, that should be everything. Oh, yeah! If you're a parent, mission president, priesthood leader, or ward member, you might be interested in the guides I made for you in the back.

Any last minute questions?

No?

Alrighty then, onward ho!

Top Left: St. Stephen's Basilica. Top Right: My little MTC district together again for the first time since my parents came to pick me up from the MTC (the first time I came home). Bottom Left: My stellar trainer, Nestor Nővér, who had the perspective to help me continue to work as best I could until the end, but also encouraged me to go home and do good there. She even came to visit me in Arizona when she finished her mission! Bottom Right: Standing with Magdi, a wonderful convert from Pest, who would patiently work with me on my Hungarian. Everyday she did personal and language study, just like the missionaries. June through July 2009.

Top Left: My new reality as we tried to get a diagnosis. November 2009. Top Right: A few of the sweet members who surprised me at the mission home my last night. (The moment my amazing trainer heard I would be going home, she made a ton of phone calls to ask these members to come say goodbye. I will never be able to thank her enough for that service.) August 2009. Bottom Left: Edit and I when I was able to visit Hungary in June 2013. I share a bit of Edit's incredible work in chapter 5, "How Do I Find Meaning Again?" Bottom Right: My first day of work at the Church Office Building. Little did I know how many opportunities would be given to me to share my mission story and the struggles of early RMs. During this time I started writing this book and conducting interviews. January 2014.

"All your losses will be made up to you in the resurrection, provided you continue faithful. By the vision of the Almighty I have seen it."

—Joseph Smith

DOES ANYONE SURVIVE THIS?

I remember the day I arrived home. After my plane landed, I climbed into a wheelchair and made my way through Salt Lake International Airport. I saw my parents standing there, completely in a daze ... just as I was.

This was the second time I came home early from my mission. Last time I had the hope of somehow returning to my mission in Hungary. This time my return was permanent, and it hurt my heart like none other.

As I got into my parents' van and we started the long drive home to my tiny hometown of Paulden, Arizona, I remembered the only other missionary who had ever come home early to my home ward. Last I heard, he had moved away and was inactive in the Church.

I couldn't help but sit in our minivan and wonder, "Does ANYONE survive coming home early?"

———

Were you feeling lost right off the plane too?

Chandler Crockett
"I went straight from the airport to the hospital, so there wasn't really any transition time. I immediately went from being a missionary to not being a missionary. There was no transition back into normal life. The hardest thing for me is that I was only in the mission for three weeks, so I sometimes wonder, did I even make a

difference? Does anyone remember me, that I was there? Did I leave an impression?"

Darcy Lethco
"I was afraid that I would sink into this hole of just being depressed, not doing anything, being idle. I was afraid of being treated like an invalid, not wanting to go back on my mission, losing the fire."

Amy Van Heel
"Was healing possible for everyone but me? Could everyone but me have their 'happily ever after'? I felt like I would never heal."

Chelsea Jones
"To be completely honest, my biggest thought was how disappointed my parents would be, especially my mom. That was probably my biggest worry: 'Oh my goodness, they spent all this money and have been sending all these great messages about how their faith is being built and how great their life is because I'm on a mission, but now I'm cutting that short.'"

Hunter Jones
"It was hard to feel good at first because I knew coming home was going to be awkward and weird for everyone. And that's what scared me the most, just the idea of coming home early."

Jenny Rollins
"It was a really hard adjustment. Every time I'd see a missionary, I'd cry. Once I tried to buy a plane ticket. I hadn't had a baptism my whole mission, and one of our converts decided to get baptized two

weeks after I got home. I almost bought a plane ticket with money I didn't have to fly back, just because I wanted to be there. It was really, really difficult."

Kiana Lindmeir
"I was an emotional wreck, and I just cried for days."

Britt Barlow
"Honestly, I was worried about my testimony because I thought, 'This is going to be terrible. I'm going home because I'm sick and I can't really do work and I'm going to come home to my family, which is fine, but too much of your family can be hard.' The other part that was really hard for me (it's still hard for me) was thinking, 'No one's going to remember me from my mission because I was only there for three months. Will the ward members remember me? I was only in one ward. Did I really make any difference?'"

———

I don't share these stories to bum you out, but to show that you're not alone in having these fears. Every single one of us early RMs have had them.

You're Not Alone

As I began writing this book, it seemed as though every few days I would hear from someone who had just come home from their mission or a family member of an early RM. I was overwhelmed by the powerful survey responses from thousands of early-returned missionaries and the incredible sincerity of the many I had the opportunity to interview.

In all of my interviews, I learned something very quickly: we're a tenacious bunch.

No one ever expects to come home early. Not one of you left for your mission saying, "Bye, Mom. See you in two weeks!" Yet, that's what happened. Everything you expected about your mission got turned upside down. But you're still here. You're reading this book, tenaciously fighting to take the next step.

> *Courtney Dickson*
> "On the plane I just realized, 'There are two ways to manage this: I can become completely bitter and angry at God, or I can just trust in Him—I can be frustrated about my situation, or I can just embrace it.' I decided, 'I'm just going to trust in Him. And I'm going to embrace it.'"

Every person I interviewed shared with me their worst fears on the flight home, their struggles with going to church the first week, their battles with feelings of failure, and, most importantly, what they learned during this experience.

As crazy as it sounds, with every interview and with every response, I felt some relief; I wasn't the only one feeling these things. I wasn't the only one terrified of what happens next. I wasn't the only one who felt like my testimony had disappeared. I wasn't the only one who felt a little betrayed by my Heavenly Father.

I hope you feel the same relief as you read these responses.

Our Enemies Come in All Shapes and Sizes

A pivotal moment in my healing was when I read Doctrine and Covenants 124:49 in the context of being an early-returned missionary.

> *Verily, verily, I say unto you, that when I give a commandment to any of the sons of men to do a work unto my name, and those sons of men go with all their might and with all they have to perform that work, and cease not their diligence, and <u>their enemies come upon them and hinder them from performing that work</u>, behold, it behooveth me to <u>require that work no more at the hands of those sons of men, but to accept of their offerings</u>.*

The enemies that hindered our work on the mission may have come as depression, a disease, a family tragedy at home, an addiction, fear of the unknown, a broken foot, or a variety of other reasons.

The Lord knew this would happen. He knew that your enemies would come and hinder you from performing His work. But you are reading this book. You are ceasing not in your diligence by searching for ways to survive this trial. And, as Nephi says, the Lord "shall prepare a way" (1 Nephi 3:7) for you.

There are many verses other than Doctrine and Covenants 124:49 that helped me during this time. I will share them with you throughout this book. Every early RM I spoke with shared at least one verse or talk that brought them hope.

———

What scriptures or talks helped you hang in there?

Marissa Hedelius

1 Nephi 11:17

And I said unto him: I know that he loveth his children; nevertheless, I do not know the meaning of all things.

> "I felt like that was talking to me directly. I didn't know why I had to get hurt, why I was home when I so badly wished I was in Alaska, but I did know that God loved me, and because of that, whatever happened would be okay even if that meant I wasn't going to return."

Britt Barlow

"The Currant Bush," by Elder Hugh B. Brown

Look, little currant bush, I am the gardener here, and I know what I want you to be. I didn't intend you to be a fruit tree or a shade tree. I

24

want you to be a currant bush, and some day, little currant bush,
when you are laden with fruit, you are going to say, "Thank you, Mr.
Gardener, for loving me enough to cut me down, for caring enough
about me to hurt me."
"Lord, I Believe," by Elder Jeffrey R. Holland:
If your faith is a little tested in this or any season, I invite you to lean
on mine.

Hunter Jones
Doctrine and Covenants 84:88
And whoso receiveth you, there I will be also, for I will go before your
face. I will be on your right hand and on your left, and my Spirit
shall be in your hearts, and mine angels round about you, to bear you
up.

Micaela Rice
Doctrine and Covenants 18:15
And if it so be that you should labor all your days in crying
repentance unto this people, and bring, save it be one soul unto me,
how great shall be your joy with him in the kingdom of my Father!
2 Timothy 4:7
I have fought a good fight, I have finished my course, I have kept the
faith.

> "I actually went and wrote down quotes and scriptures in
> the front of my Book of Mormon so that I can go and turn
> there whenever I feel discouraged."

Chelsea Jones

"Receiving, Recognizing, and Responding to the Promptings of the Holy Ghost," by Elder David A. Bednar

> "Basically he's talking about when we're thinking about impressions and we're wondering, 'Is it really from the Spirit or is that just me thinking about it?' Most likely it was from the Lord, kind of guiding you to where you needed to go. And that has helped me to stay on the path."

Kiana Lindmeir

"Lessons from Liberty Jail," by Elder Jeffrey R. Holland

Parker Tyler

Doctrine and Covenants 6:21

I am Jesus Christ. ... I am the light which shineth in darkness.

> "We're going to find Christ throughout these times, but we have to look for Him."

Courtney Dickson

Mormon Message: "Mountains to Climb"

> "It came out right when I came home, and one of the stories in the video is of a family in Brazil. And I would just watch that and cry. And I thought, 'Okay, this [my coming home early] is a mountain to climb!'"

Ether 12:37

And because thou hast seen thy weakness thou shalt be made strong.

> "I thought, 'Heavenly Father, I can see all of my weaknesses!! So I'm ready—I'm ready for you to show me

the strong part! I'm ready!' And that gave me strength. I still struggled, but it's become a helpful thing. I feel like I'm *just* figuring it out, like 'Oh, *that's* what He means about being strong by seeing my weaknesses."

Doctrine and Covenants 78:17–18

Verily, verily, I say unto you, ye are little children, and ye have not as yet understood how great blessings the Father hath in his own hands and prepared for you; and ye cannot bear all things now; nevertheless, be of good cheer, for I will lead you along. The kingdom is yours and the blessings thereof are yours, and the riches of eternity are yours.

Darcy Lethco

Job 23:10

When he hath tried me, I shall come forth as gold.

Psalm 11:5

The Lord trieth the righteous.

3 Nephi 21:10

But behold, the life of my servant shall be in my hand; therefore they shall not hurt him, although he shall be marred because of them. Yet I will heal him, for I will show unto them that my wisdom is greater than the cunning of the devil.

Megan

Doctrine and Covenants 6:34, 36–37

Therefore, fear not, little flock; do good; let earth and hell combine against you, for if you are built upon my rock, they cannot prevail. ... Look unto me in every thought; doubt not, fear not. Behold the wounds which pierced my side, and also the prints of the nails in my hands and feet; be faithful, keep my commandments, and ye shall inherit the kingdom of heaven. Amen.

"[This was] the scripture that I chose for my mission plaque. It is amazing to see how fitting that scripture truly was for my experience and the trials that came with it. I still think of this scripture often, and I am grateful for the love that I feel from Heavenly Father and Jesus Christ when I read it. Wherever we are, we can serve our Lord and Savior. We are not loved more or less for serving or not serving a full-time mission. The Lord knows our hearts and our minds. ... He loves us so much!"

Madison Stevenson

"The Currant Bush" by Elder Hugh B. Brown

"As time passed and things started to fall into place, I realized that God was in charge and that He knew this was going to be hard for me, but He also knew that it was going to push me to my absolute limit. I realized that God needed me to grow and I was done growing on my mission. I felt so much peace knowing that God knew me so well He even knew what trials to give me. He loved me enough to hurt me and cut me down just so I could grow bigger!"

Christie Hansen

Proverbs 3:5–6

Trust in the Lord with all thine heart; and lean not unto thine own understanding. In all thy ways acknowledge him, and he shall direct thy paths.

"This scripture reminds me that though I may not understand why I am going through something, there is a reason and as long as I go with HIM, I will go to places I never imaged."

Chandler Crockett
Doctrine and Covenants 121:7–10
"God talks to Joseph Smith and just says, 'Your suffering is not that bad. Job had it way worse. Peace be unto you my son, your suffering is just for a short time.' And that really helped me a lot to understand that this suffering is just for a short time."

Jenny Rollins
"Like A Broken Vessel," by Elder Jeffrey R. Holland
"I think I connected with this talk a lot because people couldn't see my symptoms so they didn't understand. I listened to it every day for a long time. I felt like I was broken. I couldn't even go out with the missionaries. I tried, but I couldn't go for very long. I couldn't do anything except sit around and do puzzles. So I heard that talk and I realized that there is a balm in Gilead and there is hope and happiness and that broken isn't bad, you know? It's a tool for you to learn to be humble and learn to rely on God. And God loves broken things."
"Lead, Kindly Light," *Hymns,* no. 97
"The entire time that I was dealing with this, in the hospital rooms, I would just sing 'Lead, Kindly Light' because I didn't know what was happening. It was all dark. I didn't

know where I was going, I didn't know what the future held and I didn't know if I was going to have a permanently disabled life. So I sang that song to myself all the time. It's become one of my favorites."

Amy Van Heel
"An High Priest of Good Things to Come," by Elder Jeffrey R. Holland

"As my favorite quote says, 'Don't give up. ... Don't you quit. You keep walking. You keep trying. There is help and happiness ahead. ... You keep your chin up. It will be all right in the end. Trust God and believe in good things to come. ... Some blessings come soon, some come late, but for those who embrace the gospel of Jesus Christ, *they come*.'"

I would like to add a few more quotes and verses that have helped me as well (including *many* from President Monson):

President Thomas S. Monson
"Good timber does not grow with ease. The stronger the wind, the stronger the trees."

President Dieter F. Uchtdorf
"Your path will at times be difficult. But I give you this promise: ... rise up and follow in the footsteps of our Redeemer and Savior, and one day you will look back and be filled with eternal gratitude that you chose to trust the Atonement and its power to lift you up and give you strength."

President Thomas S. Monson
"Our Heavenly Father...knows that we learn and grow and become stronger as we face and survive the trials. ...such difficulties allow us to change for the better, to rebuild our lives in the way our Heavenly Father teaches us, and to become something different from what we were."

Elder M. Russell Ballard
"No matter how difficult the trail...we can take comfort in knowing that others before us have borne life's most grievous trials and tragedies by looking to heaven."

President Thomas S. Monson
"Only the master knows the depths of our trials. He alone offers us eternal peace in that time of adversity. He alone touches our tortured souls."

Alma 36:3
"Whosoever put their trust in God shall be supported in their trials, and their troubles, and their afflictions, and shall be lifted up at the last day."

President Thomas S. Monson
"Doubt destroys, faith fulfills."

Sister Neill F. Marriott
"A meek heart accepts the trial and the waiting for that time of healing and wholeness to come."

President Thomas S. Monson
"You will one day stand aside and look at your difficult times, and you will realize that He was always there beside you."

Sheri L. Dew
"Lucifer whispers that life's not fair and that if the gospel were true, we would never have problems or disappointments. ...The gospel isn't a guarantee against tribulation. That would be like a test with no questions. Rather, the gospel is a guide for maneuvering through the challenges of life with a sense of purpose and direction."

Alma 26:27
"Now when our hearts were depressed, and we were about to turn back, behold the Lord comforted us, and said...bear with patience thine afflictions, and I will give unto you success."

Elder Neal A. Maxwell
"The acceptance of the reality that we are in the Lord's loving hands is only a recognition that we have never really been anywhere else."

———

For years, I would not (perhaps could not) share my story. I didn't want to talk about the mission, and I thought I was one of the few out there who "failed" my mission. I had no idea how many of us early RMs are out there.

But over time and with the amazing enabling power of the Savior's Atonement, I am now ready to share my story and the stories of other missionaries to help those of you getting off the plane today, this month, or this year.

You Served a Mission. Period.

Before we proceed, I have to admit something.

After the mission, I didn't feel like I could say I was a returned missionary. After all, it wasn't exactly made up of 100% pleasant memories, and I felt that I had let the Lord down ... really, I felt like I 'blew it.' In my perspective, a seven-month mission didn't count.

Six years later, I've realized something (and please trust me on this):

Whether you were on your mission for 1 year and 11 months or 24 hours before coming home early, **you served a mission.** Period. You got the call, you chose to go, and that's why you can say, WITH CONFIDENCE, that you are an RM.

Answering an Early RM's Question

"When someone asks you if you've served a mission, you say yes. You do not need to follow that up with 'But it was only four months.' Just forget that part and say yes, you served a mission. And be proud of the time that you spent.

"Most mission presidents, maybe most missionaries have quoted it who know anything about those wonderful, wonderful days in England when legions of people joined the Church through that early apostolic mission.

"Well, that mission only lasted eight months. Now, apparently nobody said at that point that Brother Kimball had to go for two years. Also, I suppose nobody said later on that other people went for four or five years. But the point is, cherish the service you rendered. Be grateful for the opportunity to have testified, to have been out in the name of the Lord, to have worn that missionary name plaque."

—Elder Jeffrey R. Holland

HAVE I FAILED THE LORD?

Coming home early can be traumatic. It is unexpected and often happens quickly without much warning. It was years before I allowed myself to call it a traumatic experience, and I think, as a result, it took longer for me to work through the grief cycle.

What Is the Grief Cycle?

As you process coming home, it is vital that you <u>let</u> yourself grieve the loss of the mission you anticipated. Grieving is no fun, but it is essential to your healing. You may find that your parents will be grieving as well in their own way. Don't force yourself into any of the stages and be careful not to expect yourself to handle this better than you are. Coming home can be a trauma for some—give yourself the time (months or years) to come to terms with this.

Denial, anger, bargaining, depression, and acceptance are the five most common stages of grief. You may not go through them in this order, and you may jump back and forth from one to another, but coming to understand these five steps will help if you can recognize where you are in the process.

Denial

Denial helps us survive during a time of grief or loss. Life seems to make no sense and we turn off emotionally to keep the feelings that overwhelm us at bay. To be honest, I don't remember much of my denial stage. Mostly, I woke up and laid in bed all day. Yes, rest was vital for my body to heal, but my mind also needed a break. Everything was blurry and dark during this stage. I just did my best to exist. You may feel similarly, or denial may come in other forms, perhaps even feeling an increase in energy and keeping busy to distract yourself.

Anger

A necessary part of healing is feeling your emotions. If you're like me, you may struggle with *letting* yourself truly feel anger and making your way through this stage. My anger was mainly focused at myself, feeling that I was the one at fault for coming home. There were a few times, however, that I felt angry at God. I felt betrayed that He would take my mission, of all things, away from me and that He was (seemingly) leaving me to make my way through it alone. I was in pain and didn't have a healthy way to release that anger, so sometimes it came out at my parents who were doing all they could to help me find answers to my health problems. The point is that I needed to feel that anger rather than try to stuff it down or ignore it because it seemed like the wrong thing to feel during this time.

Bargaining

You may find yourself bargaining with the Lord. You may want everything to go back to the way it was before. You may think "If only I had …" or "What if …?" I remember the day before I flew home from the mission, praying to the Lord and asking for a miracle. I made promises to Him that if He would let me stay, I would do anything for Him. I was sure that if I made the right bargain, I would be healed and be able to stay.

One sister was companions with three different sisters over six months who had to come home early. She said that it was the hardest part of her mission to see them struggle physically, emotionally and spiritually and listen to their prayers as they pled with the Lord to be able to stay. She said she watched them lose hope and adopt the feeling of "It's because I'm not good enough" when that was simply untrue.

It is not wrong to ask Him that things might be different, after all, even Jesus Christ pled that the cup might pass, but it helps to recognize that this is often one of the stages of the grieving process and just because our circumstances do not change, does not mean that the Lord isn't listening to our sincere prayers.

> *Sheri Dew*
> "I pleaded with the Lord to change my circumstances ... instead, he changed my heart."

Depression

Many early RMs experience depression after coming home. You may wonder if things will ever get better. You may wonder if you'll ever feel okay about how your mission turned out. I certainly wondered if I would ever be able to tell someone about my mission without feeling terrible loss.

While short-term depression is normal after a loss or trauma, seriously consider going to a counselor or therapist if the depression seems to be worsening or is continually returning.

> *Britt Barlow*
> "I did pretty well in the beginning. When they released me, I didn't cry. I think it all felt surreal. But my bishop said, 'Britt, this is the thing: I don't want you to expect yourself to be fine, because you're not going to be. You're so sick. It's okay to be depressed.' Which was something so foreign to me. He said, 'When your body doesn't work, it's extremely frustrating, and a natural consequence is to be depressed.'"

Acceptance

Acceptance doesn't necessarily mean that you feel great (or even okay) about what happened. For most, acceptance is learning to live in this new reality. It's hard for me to identify when I started feeling acceptance, but I do know that it took years before I finally accepted that I may have this health problem for the rest of my life. In the chapter *How Do I Find Meaning Again?*, I talk about setting goals. I think that when I started looking forward to reaching my goals again, I finally started to accept that I was home for good and would find a way to live with my new health problems.

A good rule of thumb as you grieve is best expressed by President Dieter F. Uchtdorf:

> "It is good advice to slow down a little, steady the course, and focus on the essentials when experiencing adverse conditions."

Doesn't the Lord Protect His Missionaries?

In the course of writing this book, I interviewed or read the survey responses of more than 1,000 early-returned missionaries. Some said they felt a confirmation that they should come home, while others (like me) most certainly did not. I fought to stay on my mission even though I was beyond being able to function as a missionary. I just could not conceive that coming home early could in ANY way be part of the Lord's plan. After all, doesn't the Lord protect His missionaries?

Last year I had the opportunity to share my story on *Don't Stop Sargeant*, a website encouraging hope for early RMs and members with mental illness. I entitled the post, "The Lord Protects His Missionaries" because I used to find that phrase so ironic after my time in the mission field. It has since become representative of my healing process.

In my post, I wrote:

> "I still have days when I kinda wish I had a 'normal' mission simply because it would have been an easier road in some ways—but now I am better able to judge my mission on the content rather than the length of my service. I know that He is aware of the time I was in Hungary and my heart's desires. And I now know that the Lord does protect His missionaries, just maybe in different ways than I expected. He protected my heart during this growing experience. He protected my fragile testimony during this time. He protected me."

At first I was confused that the Lord did not protect me and allow me to serve a year and a half. But with time I came to realize that the Lord was with me throughout this experience.

A Change of Perspective

Let's imagine that you decided to go on a humanitarian trip to Zimbabwe. You saved up your money for years, your anticipation grew, and you knew you'd make a difference. The trip was supposed to be three months, but unfortunately you got sick and had to come home after one month. How would you feel? I can tell you how I would feel! I would be so bummed and definitely think once or twice, "Life isn't fair!" But then I would move forward. Life happens, and it didn't work out. Everyone around me, including myself, would just be excited that I got to go at all.

Now, don't get me wrong—going on a mission is definitely a bit more than going on a short humanitarian trip. But doing the following activity really helped me look at my mission in a different way. Try this little exercise for a few minutes:

You saved up your money to go on a mission, you were excited, and you committed to the Lord that you would make a difference. But life happened and now you're home. Bummer! Big bummer. Think about it—if you were on that short humanitarian trip to Zimbabwe and came home early, would you feel like you failed? Probably not. You had the wonderful opportunity to serve the people of Kentucky or Cape Verde or Hungary or the MTC and give your all to the Lord. How blessed we were to be able to go at all!

One of the mothers of an early RM told me that when she and her husband heard the news, they were in shock. When their neighbor, who was not a member, heard that their son was coming home, he said, "I bet you're so excited to see him again!" They tried to explain their shock and dismay, but the neighbor said something along the lines of, "If I had a son who had decided to give God two years of his life, I wouldn't care if he came home early. How many young people actually choose to do something like that?" This mother and father realized that this was an incredible thing to make that kind of commitment, whether it ended up being for two years or a few months.

Aaron Olsen, an early RM wrote an article for *LDS Living* entitled, "When a Missionary Returns Early." He made clear point for all of us (and those around us) to remember:

"Every early release missionary should be proud of his or her contribution and willing heart. I was told an analogy that has struck me inside again and again. In the military, the view of completing missions and of wounded comrades is quite different from our view of similar situations in religious missions. If soldiers rush into battle and are wounded on their first mission or 50th mission, they are treated the same. They are given medals. They are applauded for their service, no matter how long. Their brothers and sisters at arms risk their own lives to rescue and restore those soldiers to their homes. No one looks at them differently. No one says, 'Well, you didn't really help the war efforts, did you?' or 'Toughen up, man. It's just a bullet.' These brave men and women are honored and respected for their service. So should it be with missionaries. We were willing to go where the Lord asked. Sometimes we get hurt. All we ask for is acceptance and love. We return with dread, hoping our partial offering will still be accepted to those we care about most. My hope is that every missionary will be loved and respected. With your understanding and support, it can happen."

Does My Mission Even Count?

A meteorologist once asked if a butterfly flapping its wings could, with time, start a chain of reactions that resulted in a tornado. This became known as "the butterfly effect."

I think it is difficult for us early RMs to know if our missions made a difference. After all, many of us can't use the traditional indicators like number of baptisms, awesome conversion stories, receiving special callings in difficult areas, training a greenie, etc., to feel like we left the mission better than when we got there. When we look at these indicators, we may feel that we have failed the mission.

But we have no idea what the ripple effect of our short missions may be. This may sound a little corny, but maybe our missions were the butterfly of the tornado! Who knows? The Lord knows and He called us to our missions for a reason. And while we may never know what difference we made, I hold to the hope that in the next life, we'll be able to see exactly why we were called to that area for that amount of time.

> *Micaela Rice*
> "My bishop told me in the MTC that God can do mighty miracles, but He works with thousands of small ones. Little words you said. Smiles you gave. Just having been there. He said, 'I promise you that there are people who have thanked God for sending you to them, maybe even because of a comment you never thought about again.' Your mission mattered. And it still does."

Length vs. Content

For years after my mission, I often got a little too caught up in what *I* thought a mission should be: 18 months of serving the Lord all day, every day, without pausing for a breath. My mission became seven months of serving the Lord all day, every day, without pausing for a breath (except at the end when the walls came a-tumblin' down). The only real difference in these two sentences is the number of months. That's it.

I know this is a tough topic, and I definitely would have had a hard time reading this five years ago, but here's what I've figured out in the last couple of years: I can't judge my mission on the length, but I can focus on the content. Try to think about the *content* of your mission for a moment.

Rather than saying one (or all) of the following:
- I never had a tie-burning ceremony
- I never left the MTC
- I never even saw a baptism
- I never made it to a transfer
- I never got to say goodbye to the people I served and loved
- I never had a great companion (or a lousy companion)

Maybe judge the content of your mission this way:
- Did I have Spirit-inspiring moments during my pre-mission preparation, in the MTC, or in the field?
- Did I meet people (companions, members, leaders, or investigators) who changed my life?

- Was I willing to serve the Lord? (Obviously yes, or you never would have gone.)

I feel like the last question is the most important. You turned in your papers. You chose to go on your mission. You were called of the Lord. Period.

I have been reading a lot of books lately on being efficient in the workplace. There is a book called *The Mormon Way of Doing Business* that takes the advice from members of the Church like the founder of JetBlue, the dean of Harvard Business School, and the CEO of Dell. And one of the things all of them say is that the number of hours someone works has little or nothing to do with their productivity. What that means is that someone who is dedicated and smart can sometimes put in five hours and get more done than someone who works a nine-to-five job.

So if we apply this concept to our missions, does length (the number of hours you were in the field) determine the quality of your mission? Eighteen months and twenty-four months are the expected length of all missions, BUT does that mean your mission is any less than someone who had the opportunity to stay the whole time?

> *Britt Barlow*
> "When people asked me if I served a mission, I say yes, and I don't bring up that I only served for three months. My stake president asked me, 'Do you know that our former stake president came home early from his mission, and he never

went back out? Your mission counts, no matter how small it was or how short of time. You finished your mission.' Hearing that from a priesthood leader really helped. I did feel like I served a mission."

You and the 73%

Get ready to be shocked. According to a study made by Utah Valley University, 73% of early-returned missionaries feel like they failed. This is across the board, no matter the reason for coming home. **73%.** So there is a good chance that if you're reading this chapter, you have feelings of failure.

The good news is that you're not alone. You and I and the other 73% understand what it's like.

These feelings are part of losing something really precious to you. You and I dreamed of our missions for a long time and planned for them for a long time. We can't expect to lose them and immediately say, "Well, shucks ... Okay, back to watching movies, dating, and sleeping in!"

My friend Ryan Freeman, who is an early RM, shared this with me:

> "It wasn't until I realized how often our definition
> of success sets us up for failure that I found peace.
> Our definition of success is different from God's."

I love how Ryan said, "Our definition of success is different from God's." Pray to the Lord to feel peace about the failure you feel. Only He can help you recognize what was out of your control and *if* there is something you need to repent of. Only He can help you understand what HIS standard of success is.

———

Did you struggle with feelings of failure after the mission?

Micaela Rice
"YES! And sometimes I still do. That is Satan's biggest tool to use against early RMs. When I start feeling like a failure, I try to do one of four things: First, I go talk to people from my mission. That makes me feel like I really went and the people always make me feel loved and missed. Second, I read my mission journal and look at pictures. That is proof right there that I did serve and that I accomplished what the Lord needed me to. Third, I get a blessing. This usually helps me to feel at peace and know that it was part of the Lord's plan. Fourth, I go to the temple. This reminds me of my covenants I have made and that I still have many other missions in store for me."

Kiana Lindmeir
"I'm the kind of person that if I put my mind to something, I do it. But I remember coming home and feeling like a failure. And seeing my siblings go off on their missions was hard because then I

thought, 'Oh my goodness, they're going to do a whole mission without coming home, and I've already failed.'"

————

You and I have no idea what the Lord had in mind for our missions.

Here's the thing: you have no idea what the Lord had in mind for your mission. He may have had a shorter mission in mind for you that included some hefty trials. I guess I've realized that my whole pre-mission life I *thought* my sacrifice to the Lord would be to go on an 18-month mission away from my family, knocking on doors in rain or shine, and being rejected. Instead, my sacrifice became coming home after a seven-month mission. Whew. Not what I planned ... at all. I never thought that when I got my answer to go on a mission that I was really getting an answer to go on a short mission and come home. Even as I write this section, it's hard to put it on paper; it's a topic that is very tender for me, but I really want you to know what I've learned in this experience. It's what I wish I would have known all those years ago.

> *Britt Barlow*
> "A *huge* thing for me was, 'Am I making this up? Because a mission is so hard, am I just making this up so that I can get home?' That was the biggest thing, the idea that if I had more faith or if I worked harder or if I thought of some solution, I'd be able to stay and that it was me not wanting

to serve a mission. Until that moment where I prayed about it, I never thought it was Heavenly Father's will. I thought it was me being weak."

Focusing on Your Brick

There is a story of a monastery in Tibet that monks have been building for 1200+ years. Each monk is in charge of making one to two bricks *over the course of their entire lifetime*. Each brick is lovingly made as perfect as possible and placed on the walls of bricks that have been created by other monks for over a millennium. Each monk knew that they would never see the monastery completed, nor would each generation after them, but that was not the point. All that mattered is how they made their brick.

Okay, so I have to ask:

Do you think we could build like this in the good ol' USA? We like completing our building projects in rush time, forking out the money to outsource the work so that it can be completed as cheaply and quickly as possible. We would NEVER be able to sit peacefully, knowing that this building would not be built in our lifetime, our children's lifetime, or our great-great-great-great grandchildren's lifetimes.

I'm sure you're probably thinking: "Okay .... What does this have to do with the price of beans? What's your point?"

I'm going to share one more story, then I'll spill the beans ... [and yes, that was a pun...]

I came across a book once called *The Power of Passion*. It was about two men, Alan Hobson and Jamie Clarke, who climbed Mount Everest ... almost. Actually, they never reached the top in the course of the book because things kept happening and they had to pull out and go home. Twice. The End.

Now be honest with me—what are you thinking right now? Does part of you think, "Ummm, Destiny, that sounds like kind of a lame story. Did you even finish the book?"

You can bet that *The Power of Passion* was **not** a New York Times Best Seller. As Americans, we want to read about the guys who make it to the top. The team that beats all odds to win the Super Bowl. The 12-year-old gymnast who was a runt as a kid and won gold at the Olympics. We don't want to "waste our time" reading about two guys who couldn't cut it. I mean, what's the point of reading the book at all?

Well, I read the book. And I actually loved it.

It took me a few chapters to stop thinking, "Sheesh, guys, why did you waste your time writing this book? Why didn't you wait until you eventually made it to the top of Everest before writing this?" My perspective changed after reading the following story.

On their second journey up to Everest (keep in mind they had already failed at achieving their goal once), they were within a matter of feet of reaching the top when someone in their group started suffocating from water in his lungs. They were able to stabilize him and, although they were only one day away from reaching the top, they began preparing for the rescue down the mountain.

> "We turned our backs on the summit and we went after our friend. Sometimes in life, there are more important things than getting to the goal."

Every single member of the team was exhausted, and they were worried about getting their friend to camp in time. They looked down the glacier and "saw a snake of lights winding its way up towards the bottom of the slope." It took them a moment to realize that

> "It was the headlamps of other climbers coming to help. ... They were sacrificing their own energy and summit chances to rescue someone in the middle of the night, someone who wasn't even from their own country or team.

> "A satisfaction came over [us] far more meaningful than either of us had felt on any summit.

> "Sometimes it takes more courage and strength to turn your back on a goal than to continue."

As I read this account, I realized two things. First, the people that always say "find joy in the journey" are right! These guys spent *years* preparing to get to the point on Everest where they had to turn around. But then was their trip over? Could they go home and sulk? No! They still had *weeks* of climbing back down, with the peak of Everest in sight but out of grasp. Talk about frustrating! They had to discover the simple joys of the journey to keep from going crazy. Second, these men had to give up their Everest goal twice because of circumstances they could not control. They could only change their perspectives. And, as they said, that often takes more strength and courage than reaching the actual goal.

I'm the kind of person that will do anything to summit that peak or win that race. Achieving something is one of the best feelings in the world! But sometimes I find it hard to enjoy the journey when the journey stinks. I mean, I wanted to be that missionary who finished a year and a half of serving with honor; who walked [maybe even strutted a bit?] off the plane with tons of family in the airport terminal to welcome me home. Didn't you? I wanted to be one of "those" missionaries. I expected a perfectly normal mission and I wanted to be a perfect missionary.

> *President Gordon B. Hinckley*
> "Please don't nag yourself with thoughts of failure. Do not set goals far beyond your capacity to achieve. Simply do what you can do, in the best way you know, and the Lord will accept of your effort."

And that's the thing—every day I want to be a perfect being and push myself to reach that goal. I forget that we are not on earth to be perfect, we are here to be _____. [You're all missionaries. Fill in the blank!]

Exactly! We're here to be *tested*. And tested means doing hard things. Tested means doing things beyond what we think we can do. Tested means a LOT of practice (and a lot of mistakes) before doing something right. But sometimes (okay, most of the time), I forget that part and still plan on being pretty darn close to perfect by the end of my life.

But wait a second, what does this mean when I mess up? What happens when I make mistakes and fall flat on my face? What if I wake up one morning and feel further away from being perfect than before my mission? That means I beat myself up for not reaching the summit. I beat myself up for not building a humongous monastery today.

> *Amy Van Heel*
> "Remember, it is not about perfection but progress."

Remember when Paul pleads with the Lord three times (at least) to remove his "thorn in the flesh" (2 Cor. 12:7)? A thorn in the flesh can be a weakness. From what I can tell, the Lord does *not* remove his weakness but instead says one of my favorite verses of scripture: "My grace is sufficient for thee: for my strength is made perfect in weakness" (2 Cor. 12:9).

We have to step back and look at the big picture. Heavenly Father wants us to become perfect. He wants us each to build a beautiful monastery. He has allowed, in His grace, eons of time to give us the time we need to become perfect. For this earth life, rather than assuming that we need to build our monastery before we die, we have to remember to focus on our brick. Our monasteries of perfection will take millennia to build. We have to remember that some of our "thorns in the flesh" are here for a while, and we should spend our *lifetimes* working on improving in that weak area step-by-step. We shouldn't expect ourselves to build our bricks in record time—in a week or a month or a year. Some of our weaknesses will just take time to overcome.

That's where "endure to the end" comes in. "He that is faithful and endureth shall overcome the world" (Doctrine and Covenants 63:47 [and verse 20]). The Lord knows that it may take several trips to reach the top of Everest and expects that it probably won't happen in this lifetime. But He has given us *grace* to cover the mistakes we make as we learn to navigate life. He allows weakness as an opportunity for us to become humble and realize how much we need His grace as we slowly build our brick.

> *Elder Jeffrey R. Holland*
> "My brothers and sisters, except for Jesus, there have been no flawless performances on this earthly journey we are pursuing, so while in mortality let's strive for steady improvement without obsessing over what behavioral scientists call 'toxic perfectionism.' ... Brothers and sisters, every one of us aspires to a more Christlike life than we

often succeed in living. If we admit that honestly and are trying to improve, we are not hypocrites; we are human. ... If we persevere, then somewhere in eternity our refinement will be finished and complete—which is the New Testament meaning of perfection. ... I testify of that grand destiny, made available to us by the Atonement of the Lord Jesus Christ, who Himself continued 'from grace to grace' until in His immortality He received a perfect fulness of celestial glory."

Grace is not just for serious sinners.

Prior to the mission, I always thought the word *grace* was a synonym for *mercy* and that it was for serious sinners.

What I've learned in the last six years is that grace is an enabling power available through Jesus Christ's Atonement. It's something all of us can use ... and need desperately to overcome our weaknesses.

Grace is one of my favorite topics for my scripture study. As a perfectionist who is *very* aware of my weaknesses, **grace has become a way for me to trust the Lord and take it easy on myself.** Grace allows me to learn how to walk while not feeling punished or punishing myself for falling down.

President Dieter F. Uchtdorf
"Our destiny is not determined by the number of times we stumble, but by the number of times we rise up, dust ourselves off, and move forward."

When I got home, I found out quickly that Satan was going to use every opportunity he could to remind me that I "blew it" on the mission. He made sure that I remembered all of my mistakes in the mission and tempted me like never before to fall to temptation at home. All I could think to myself was, "Not only did you come home early, Destiny, but now you're adding even more mistakes to your rap sheet!"

I didn't realize that I was in survival mode after the mission. I had been through a traumatic experience and my defenses were weak. Instead of taking it easy on myself, I made things worse by beating myself up every time I couldn't make it through church or I missed scripture study or I struggled with a temptation.

It wasn't until I heard Brad Wilcox's talk "His Grace Is Sufficient" at BYU that I realized I did not understand the Atonement of Jesus Christ. Brother Wilcox gave a great analogy about piano lessons:

> "Christ's arrangement with us is similar to a mom providing music lessons for her child. Mom pays the piano teacher. ... Because Mom pays the debt in full, she can turn to her child and ask for something. What is it? Practice! Does the child's practice pay the piano teacher? No. Does the child's practice

repay Mom for paying the piano teacher? No. Practicing is how the child shows appreciation for Mom's incredible gift. It is how he takes advantage of the amazing opportunity Mom is giving him to live his life at a higher level. Mom's joy is found not in getting repaid but in seeing her gift used—seeing her child improve. And so she continues to call for practice, practice, practice.

"If the child sees Mom's requirement of practice as being too overbearing ("Gosh, Mom, why do I need to practice? None of the other kids have to practice! I'm just going to be a professional baseball player anyway!"), perhaps it is because he doesn't yet see with Mom's eyes. He doesn't see how much better his life could be if he would choose to live on a higher plane.

"In the same way, because Jesus has paid justice, He can now turn to us and say, "Follow me" (Matthew 4:19), "Keep my commandments" (John 14:15). If we see His requirements as being way too much to ask ("Gosh! None of the other Christians have to pay tithing! None of the other Christians have to go on missions, serve in callings, and do temple work!"), maybe it is because we do not yet see through Christ's eyes. We have not yet comprehended what He is trying to make of us."

When we do our best to obey the commandments, repent, and become better people, we are not repaying Him—we are showing our appreciation for His sacrifice.

The part of Brother Wilcox's talk that really stood out to me was when he used the piano analogy to talk about grace's role in allowing us time to learn how to become perfect.

"'But Brother Wilcox, don't you realize how hard it is to practice? I'm just not very good at the piano. I hit a lot of wrong notes. It takes me forever to get it right.' Now wait. Isn't that all part of the learning process? When a young pianist hits a wrong note, we don't say he is not worthy to keep practicing. We don't expect him to be flawless. We just expect him to keep trying. Perfection may be his ultimate goal, but for now we can be content with progress in the right direction. Why is this perspective so easy to see in the context of learning piano but so hard to see in the context of learning heaven?

"Too many are giving up on the Church because they are tired of constantly feeling like they are falling short. They have tried in the past, but they always feel like they are just not good enough. They don't understand grace. ...

"... When learning the piano, are the only options performing at Carnegie Hall or quitting? No. Growth and development take time. Learning takes time. When we understand grace, we understand that God is long-suffering, that change is a process, and that repentance is a pattern in our lives. When we understand grace, we understand that the blessings of Christ's Atonement are continuous and His strength is perfect in our weakness (see 2 Corinthians 12:9). When we understand grace, we can, as it says in the Doctrine and Covenants, 'continue in patience until [we] are perfected' (Doctrine and Covenants 67:13)."

Isn't this a great analogy? I love thinking about this in terms of the first story I shared in this chapter. Our goal in this earth life is not about quickly building a huge monastery. Nor is it about being able to sit down and immediately play Chopin's *Fantaisie-Impromptu*. It's about doing the best we can to show our gratitude to our Savior and taking it easy on ourselves when our "thorns in the flesh" refuse to leave.

———

What have you learned about Jesus Christ's Atonement and grace during this process?

Kiana Lindmeir
"Something that I studied a lot when I came home was grace and the enabling power of the Savior's Atonement. And something I never knew before my mission was that Christ doesn't just make up for those sins, He's also there for us; He helps us. He enables us to do more than we could on our own. And when I came home, I was

struggling so much that honestly there was no way, I just don't think I could have gone through it. You know, I honestly believe it was because Christ was helping me and He knew I was struggling and that because I was following Him and doing all that I could, He was helping me."

Madison Stevenson
"The Atonement is not just for our mistakes. It's for our trials and pain and hard times and struggles, and as we realize that Christ already suffered those pains, we also realize it has to be part of God's plan."

Amy Van Heel
"I use to believe that the Savior's Atonement only worked for everyone besides me. I couldn't change. There was no way that I could heal. The Atonement isn't just for people who have perfect lives or don't make mistakes. The process is slow and not noticeable when you go through affliction and hardships, unless you strive to notice how the Lord has been in your life. But then you see it when you wake up one day and I realize, oh, I don't feel hopeless. Then you realize you love yourself even with your mistakes and stupid actions, and you don't dwell on those mistakes or beat yourself up for those things. You forgive yourself."

Ryan Freeman
"The Atonement is very personal, and I don't think I discovered that until I returned home. People would often ask me if I had a belief in the Savior's Atonement, implying that my difficulty was the result of unbelief. While I don't want to disregard their

experiences with the Atonement, experiences are not universal. God is able to work through many ways, and we limit Him and Christ's Atonement by describing it as another form of Tylenol. Sometimes we are carried and sometimes we are expected to go straight through a challenge."

Micaela Rice
"I learned that Christ really has suffered for everything—not just sins but any negative emotion that you have. I have learned that the Savior's Atonement is something we need to rely on daily and that if we do, we can feel peace and love from our Heavenly Father and Savior. I have learned that Christ's Atonement carries us even when we feel as if we can't go any further. And all in all, His Atonement has taught me how to trust Him and my Heavenly Father."

Chandler Crockett
"The Savior's Atonement is not just there for sin. It's there for pain. It's there for illness too. I mean, obviously I haven't been healed of my mental disorder, but just the hope and knowledge that someday I will be is very comforting."

Jenny Rollins
"I had one of my zone leaders give me a blessing when I was out in the mission. And he told me that once I understood the Atonement, I would be healed. And I took that as a literal thing and in my personal studies I studied the Atonement and I tried to get down all of the nuances and tried to understand it as best I could. And I still wasn't healed and I didn't get better. And I didn't get better for months. ... I realized that I had been studying factually the

aspects of the Atonement but I hadn't really asked for that much help. I'm independant. I think I had understood repentance but I hadn't really understood the healing power of the Savior's Atonement outside of repentance."

Christie Hansen
"Jesus' Atonement is really there to help us with anything. He helped me overcome my feelings of failure and all the other negative feelings I had when I came home. He really suffered everything. He knew exactly how I felt in all those moments and was there willing and ready to help me through it all. He loved me enough to experience my pain so that I could have help through it."

"He will not always take your afflictions from you, but He will comfort and lead you with love through whatever storm you face."

—*President Thomas S. Monson*

"For if our heart condemn us,
God is greater than our heart,
and knoweth all things."

1 John 3:20

FOR THOSE OF YOU WHO CAME HOME FOR TRANSGRESSION REASONS

Elder Jeffrey R. Holland
"God doesn't care nearly as much about where you have been as He does about where you are and, with His help, where you are willing to go."

There are many of you who have come home for reasons other than physical or emotional health. You may have an addiction that you thought you overcame before the mission. You may have unresolved sin that you weren't honest about to get on the mission. You may have broken mission rules (or let your companion break the rules). You may have committed serious sins in the field that hurt other missionaries and the members around you. With the variety of reasons you may be reading this section, you can see why there is no one-size-fits-all solution except for Jesus Christ's Atonement. It is key that you immediately meet with your bishop so that you can receive guidance and revelation specific to your situation.

Before we continue, though, I have to say something. I truly believe that you coming home from the mission early may have been one of the best decisions you could have made.

You might be thinking right now, "Destiny, you're crazy—isn't staying on the mission always the best choice?" or at least, "Destiny, you don't understand my unique situation—I really blew it, big time."

Make a deal with me. Promise me that you'll read this entire chapter before you decide to dismiss what I say or stop reading this book altogether. While only you and your bishop together know what your repentance process will look like, I hope that you will feel hope while reading this chapter.

A Step Forward

One thing is sure—whether you messed up before or during the mission, you and I both know that you had to come home. You couldn't stay in the mission. It wouldn't be right before the Lord. You'd be living a lie, which has a big impact on your ability to do His work.

> *Chelsea Jones*
> "I tried really hard not to focus on 'I disappointed my Heavenly Father.' He knows the reason I'm coming home. He understands what I'm feeling and He gets it. He's proud of me for going home if I needed to, and He's also proud of the work that I did. It's constantly telling yourself that, that is the hardest thing."

However, I have great news! Coming home can be a huge step *forward* in your life. Sometimes we make mistakes, mistakes we regret for a long time, but here's what I beg you to remember:

Coming home does not equal spiritual death.

It may feel like it at times ... maybe most of the time right now. It sure did to me. I left my mission and I honestly thought that was the worst thing I could have done in my life. You know what? It's okay to feel this way because you're feeling remorse. That can be a good thing. BUT, now is the time to show your Heavenly Father that you are not going anywhere! You're sticking it out!

President Thomas S. Monson
"Our task is to become our best selves. One of God's greatest gifts to us is the joy of trying again, for no failure ever need be final."

Think of Alma the Younger. He grew up in a wonderful home with parents who loved him and taught him the gospel and then he 'blew it' by "seeking to destroy the church" (Alma 36:6). That's one doozy of a mistake.

But was that his spiritual death? Was that the end for him? Well, ... it was really, really close, and it could have been the end if he had ignored the angel who came to tell him to straighten up his act. But here's the thing: he decided that getting chewed out by an angel was going to be his first *step forward*, not a step backward in his spiritual progression. And only through Jesus Christ was he able to make much-needed changes in his life.

There was another guy, you probably know him, who had a similar experience. Saul was killing Christians when he got a visit from an angel. Again, it wasn't a very pleasant experience, and he could have ignored the not-so-gentle prompting. He could have been like Laman and Lemuel, who saw an angel and yet continued to try to kill Nephi repeatedly throughout their lives. (I think we can agree that this is a step backwards.) But Saul decided this was his chance to utilize both the forgiving and enabling power of Jesus Christ's Atonement.

I *told* you this was great news! Think about it: you can be the next Alma the Younger or the next Paul! Coming home early may be your "rebuke by an angel" moment when you can choose to turn to the Lord for help rather than follow Laman and Lemuel's example.

> *Helaman 14:30–31*
> *For behold, ye are free; ye are permitted to act for yourselves; for behold, God hath given unto you a knowledge and he hath made you free.*
>
> *He hath given unto you that ye might know good from evil, and he hath given unto you that ye might choose life or death;* and **ye can do good and be restored unto that which is good, or have that which is good restored unto you**; *or ye can do evil, and have that which is evil restored unto you.*

This is your chance to utilize the Atonement in your life and make major changes in your life. Yes, you made a mistake. Yes, it may feel like it's the end. Yes, it will take time. (I'm sure Alma and the sons of Mosiah had to work hard to not revert to their past sins.) But honestly, this is your chance to show the Lord that you're here to stay. Set up an appointment with your bishop ASAP.

Be a Corianton

In the April 2015 *Ensign,* I read an article called "Repentance Is Real." (By the way, that whole *Ensign* issue is stuffed full of awesome articles. ... Take a look at it.) Anyways, Shauna Ikahihifo shares the same perspective that I've been talking about: you may feel like you've messed up, but you are "not beyond the mercies of our Savior's Atonement" (p. 13).

Shauna recounts the story of Corianton. If you're like me, you grew up reading about Corianton's sins on his mission. His father, Alma, calls him out on it and says "when [the Zoramites] saw your conduct they would not believe in my words" (Alma 39:11). I know it will be hard, but please take a moment to read all that Alma tells his son in chapters 39–42. But before you do that, I think it's important to know one thing: Corianton changed. In fact, he changed so much that he was called again to the work (see Alma 42:31), and it seems like he later became a leader in the Church (see Alma 49:30).

Shauna writes, "Corianton's failure to be obedient was not the end of him. Although it may have seemed to him that he had lost everything, his father, Alma, and the Savior knew otherwise. Through the Atonement of Jesus Christ, Corianton was able to repent and change course."

Chelsea Jones

"I remember praying, wanting to stay so I could still keep serving these people and still keep gaining these experiences. I had grown such a love for the people there. I didn't want to go home. But I also said, 'It's up to You. Wherever You want me to go and what You need me to do, I know it's going to be hard, but I'm going to do it.'"

Do not rationalize!

Now, I have to be careful in writing this. What I am saying will hurt you if I teach grace without repentance. There may be some of you that will be tempted to use this to rationalize your behavior in the mission field. Laman and Lemuel stopped repenting along the way and became convinced that their actions were justified. Do not rationalize!

It is critical that you remember that **before** Alma the Younger "could remember [his] pains no more," he was "racked with eternal torment"; his "soul was harrowed up to the greatest degree and racked" with the memory of his sins. He had to remember and come to terms with all of the sins he had committed *before* the healing started. "I saw that I had rebelled against my God." (Alma 36:19, 12, 13). Do not rationalize!

Please do not allow Satan to rationalize away the seriousness of your sin. At the same time, do not let Satan tell you that there is no hope. There most certainly *is* hope!

Make Your Decision Today

> *Elder Jeffrey R. Holland*
> "However late you think you are, however many chances you think you have missed, however many mistakes you feel you have made or talents you think you don't have, or however far from home and family and God you feel you have traveled, I testify that you have not traveled beyond the reach of divine love. It is not possible for you to sink lower than the infinite light of Christ's Atonement shines."

Can you do something for me? Write the phrases below on some sticky notes and put them in your journal, on your mirror, in your scriptures, on your pillow. Put them everywhere.

Coming home does not equal spiritual death.
Coming home is my step forward.

You can do this, friend. Just think about the day when you can look back on today and say, "The decision to make my mission a step forward was the best choice of my life."

> *Chelsea Jones*
> "I'm still trying to keep the same basics as on the mission. I'm still trying to wake up early, that's probably the biggest thing. I'm studying my scriptures and saying my prayers.

Praying right after I got back was really hard because I didn't feel like I deserved to talk to my Heavenly Father, which I feel like is a really common thing I've noticed in people who have posted blogs about early-returned missionaries. That's always the common factor: 'I don't deserve to talk to Him.' But once I got in the habit of doing that, it made it easier to keep going. And I'm still going to church even if it wasn't in my ward, still being in that environment and keeping myself around positive people was really the main thing."

You have the opportunity now, starting today, to prove to the Lord that this sin is not who you are. Show Him your sincerity by meeting with your bishop ASAP. Pray to the Lord for the desire to change. Speak with Him about each step you are making to turn to Him. Allow yourself to feel godly sorrow for your sins. Repent thoroughly and hold to the examples of Alma the Younger, Paul, and Corianton. Choose today to make your return your **step forward**.

"If he confess his sins before thee and me, and repenteth in the sincerity of his heart, him shall ye forgive and I will forgive him also. Yea, and as often as my people repent will I forgive them their tresspasses against me."

—*Mosiah 26:29-30*

Interview with Parker Tyler

I was supposed to go on my mission in 2011, and right after graduation I put in my mission papers to go. At the end of junior year, I had been dating somebody pretty steadily and we didn't get into the best of situations. It seemed like after I put in my mission papers, Satan was like, "Alright, you're getting a mission call, now we gotta make sure you don't go." So that's what happened.

Part of the repentance process is to make changes, and I didn't understand that at the time, really. So I didn't make those changes. I kind of got to the point where I was, like, "Well, I'm not really doing what I'm supposed to, but how hard can it be? I go on a mission and then I go home." The justification that comes into your head: "It's not *that* bad. You're not hurting anybody."

That general conference was October 2011. In the general priesthood session, Elder Holland gave his "stay within the lines" talk, "We Are All Enlisted." When he chastised all of us getting ready to go on our missions, he was like, "You need to get your act together. We need you, but we need you worthy—we can't just take you when you're doing all these things, and you can't expect to do all these things up until when you leave and then put on the name tag and expect it to have all magically disappeared." And so I sat there in that priesthood session, and I felt he was talking right to me.

So I had this pretty good discussion with myself. I was like, "You know what you need to do," and there was no escaping it.

The Wednesday after that talk, I called my bishop up. I just remember the love he showed for me when I told him these things. I remember the weight of it all immediately lifted. I still needed to do more changes, more repenting, but I felt a million times better. We postponed my mission for a year, and I received an informal disciplinary action.

At this time, my girlfriend had moved away for college, and so she'd come home a lot. It started well at first, but then we fell back again into same habits. Little by little you slip back into things.

Fast forward a year later, and I was not doing the things that I should have been doing. At this point I'm like, "I've already spent an extra year for my mission. I'm just going to go, get it over with." And so October of the following year, my mission call was reinstated, and I left two weeks after that.

I went to the MTC, and the first few days I was like, "This is great, this isn't that bad." Then we really started getting into the things that we were needing to teach, especially about repentance and eternal families. I think that was the first time it really clicked, how everything in the gospel fits together. So here I am, learning how to teach all these people how to have an eternal family, how to do all the right things so you can be together forever; and I'm not in a position that I can have that for myself.

It was the first Sunday that I was there, and you have that meeting with your branch president in the MTC. I told him the *bare* minimum. He was like, "Okay, that is something we need to take care of but that shouldn't be a huge deal. Let me talk to the MTC president and get back to you and we'll go from there." The next day, I get called to the MTC president's office and he sits me down and asks, "How are things going?"

Assuming that the branch president had already talked to him, I told him the *bare* minimum. He sits there and looks at me for a few seconds—it felt like several hours—and I just sat there. And he said, "I'm glad you told me that, but I feel like there's more." So I told him a little bit more, and the same thing happened. He's like, "That's good, but I feel there's more." But this time he said, "I want you to go back, take a few days, really think about things that you've done and then come back and talk to me." And in my mind, I'm sitting there thinking, "Take a few more days? I am *not* going to take a few more days with this—I know *exactly* all the things I've done, but I'm not going to sit with this guilt for a few more days." So I told him a little bit more, and this went back and forth for three or four times before I finally told him everything. And he looks at me and says, "*That's* what I was looking for."

And, the same thing, I still felt the guilt for it because I hadn't repented yet, but the weight of it all was still gone. He said, "I don't really know what to do exactly, so give me a few days and I'll call you back in and we'll figure out where to go from here."

A few days later he calls me back in and as we sit down, he says, "You know who sat in that chair 15 minutes ago? President Uchtdorf. I wasn't exactly sure what to do, so I talked to him about it." (I thought, "Wow, here I am, sitting in front of this man who can call the First Presidency and say, 'Hey, I don't know what to do with this missionary.'")

He said, "You're going to go home." And he looks me in the eye and he gets this really stern look on his face and says, "But if you screw it up this time, you're going to be in a whole lot of trouble." I was like, "Okay, I gotta start making some serious changes."

Having my parents come to the MTC was probably one of the worst experiences of my life. Having to look my parents in the eye, especially my mom, it was harsh to say the least.

When I got home, it was really hard. I had to do a formal disciplinary council this time around because the informal one hadn't been enough. But this time was hard because I had gone out and come back and so that was when Satan started saying, "You're a failure. You messed up and you couldn't do it." I had a friend that shook me into place and was like, "Look, yeah, you made these mistakes, so what? You're repenting of them. Don't let Satan tell you you can't do these things, because you can."

We postponed my mission another year. I stayed really busy. And I eventually left for my mission in March of '14, so 15 months after I had gone into the MTC.

Initially I felt like I still wasn't worthy to serve, even though I was, but that feeling went away the longer I was out and the more adjusted I got to the work! It was such a relief to finally be serving my mission worthily!

How did you keep focused during that 15 months at home and not let thoughts of failure overtake you?

It was really hard. The thing that probably helped me the most was I had the constant thought of the first time I was able to take the sacrament again. "How exquisite was my joy" is the best way to describe it. I was just so full of gratitude that I knew I could never repay Christ for what He did, but I knew that going on my mission was a good way to show Him gratitude.

That's the thing, some people may not be able to go back on the mission, but that doesn't make them a failure. I went because I wanted to show gratitude, but there are millions of other ways to show gratitude.

At the time I knew I still wanted to do my best to make a difference, to try to share the gospel. I decided I was going to do that through one of those anonymous Twitter accounts. I created one just to share gospel messages and try to be somewhat of a good influence even though I couldn't go on a mission. And that really helped me overcome those thoughts to be like, "Look, I *am* making a difference."

What did you learn about the Savior's Atonement and grace?

When we're following the commandments that He's given us, I think our perspective is better. We can turn to Christ and have Him help us bear things a lot better. We know where to go to get assistance, instead of thinking that we have to do it on our own.

I love the 12-step program, I mean even if you're not in an addiction or anything, the 12-step program is just the repentance process broken down into 12 steps. It is amazing for anybody, for anytime, for any situation! Heavenly Father and Jesus Christ's mercy is very apparent throughout that whole process.

How did you navigate your first Sunday back?

We hear these stories about how awful Church members can be and I think oftentimes Satan builds on that. That's what he did that with me. I got home on Monday so I had that whole week before that Sunday came and Satan was like, "Just don't go. Everyone will look at you and be like, 'Wow, you screwed up *again*?'"

My mom came down to my room to wake me up that morning because she knew I was struggling with the thought of going to church. And she's like, "Just come to sacrament meeting. You can sit between me and your dad and not talk to anybody."

That first Sunday was nothing like Satan had portrayed it in my mind.

I just remember walking in and seeing all these faces and just the love and concerned looks they had on their faces. I could feel that love, you could cut it with a knife, it was thick. Nobody said anything, nobody pointed it out, but some just gave me a hug, "It's good to see you here." I did notice a few people in the background looking at me with that look of "Oh, why is he home? He just left, what's going on?" But I remember that it didn't matter.

Those people weren't people that were super close to me anyways. And so I just remember not caring and just going into the chapel and sitting for sacrament meeting and staying for all three hours.

Just take it one hour at a time, and you can get through the first Sunday.

How did you navigate your formal disciplinary council?

Like I said, when I came home from the MTC, the first couple of weeks were fine. I felt pretty good after that first Sunday. And then I had my disciplinary council and it seemed like after that things got *really* hard. I was disfellowshipped as a result of the disciplinary council. I felt like I had screwed up so bad. This was before I really understood disfellowship and excommunication, and so I was scared. I was terrified because to me, disfellowship and excommunication were these terrible things that you would never be able to recover from.

But in that time, I really learned about mercy and how merciful disfellowship and excommunication are. I mean, we get these in our minds that these are such bad things—granted, you don't ever want to be in a situation where you're disfellowshipped or excommunicated—but if you *are* in those situations, disfellowshipped and excommunication are your way out. I believe it's Heavenly Father and Jesus Christ showing, acknowledging the fact that you are not in a position to keep covenants that you've made. But They're giving you another opportunity to work back to where you can make those covenants again. And so disfellowship is the same way, you're still technically a member of the Church, but I don't want to say that you're not expected to keep your covenants, because you are, you're still bound by them, but the Savior and Heavenly Father understand that you need some time to get to a position where you can honorably keep those covenants again. Like a probation period, you're on probation essentially.

A lot of people still have the mindset that it's punishment, but I wouldn't necessarily call it punishment, I would call it a consequence of an action that you made. We get to make choices all day long, but we don't get to choose the consequences. These consequences are for our benefit, whether we realize that or not.

Who in the scriptures did you relate to during this time?

Honestly, I felt like Alma the Younger and the prodigal son. I didn't physically leave home, but I felt like I had spiritually left, had spiritually checked out. I was still going through the motions, I was still going to church, but I felt like the prodigal son in the sense that I had left His home, taken things and said, "Thanks, I'm pretty good here" and then went the ways of the world. And so I feel like when I did come back and I did confess the wrongs that I had done, I felt almost unworthy of the love that I was being shown.

But I was still shown the love with open arms and open hearts. I almost felt like I had fallen down and He had picked me up and dusted me off and said, "Let's try again."

What do you feel changed for you?

I guess it kind of changed from the mission being something I was supposed to do because my parents expect me to do it, to something I was supposed to do because it was my priesthood obligation or priesthood duty for me to go, and then it turned into something I wanted to do because I'm grateful.

"Rely on the Lord, for only He can turn a mess into a message, a test into a testimony, a trial into a triumph, and what's broken into something beautiful."

—*Zandra Vanes*

"Even if you cannot always see that silver lining on your clouds, God can, for He is the very source of the light you seek."

—Jeffrey R. Holland

—

HOW DO I FIND
MEANING AGAIN?

—

As I walked off the plane in the United States, I couldn't help but think that I had left the most important work of my life behind in the mission field.

It took time, but I learned that there was work here at home that would bring my life meaning as well. In addition to reading my scriptures, praying, and attending church, each of the following steps on my journey was a miracle and vital to my healing.

> *Madison Stevenson*
> "My biggest fear was the thought of 'What am I going to do now?' I felt that it was almost unfair. Every other missionary knew when they were going home. They had time to have parents or siblings sign them up for college classes or contact old bosses to get their jobs back. They had a plan. I didn't. It was thrown at me, and I was so afraid of not having a plan and not knowing what was next."

1. Staying Connected

My first step to finding meaning in my life was to stay connected with the Saints and missionaries in Hungary.

For a time, my life revolved around P-days when I would receive emails from my mission trainer, Sister Nestor, and my MTC companions. (My mission president was kind enough to give them special permission to write me.)

I have to admit, sometimes it wasn't easy to read about my companions' missions or to speak with the Hungarians whom I missed so badly. But as I look back now, I realize that it was critical to my healing to hear about the miracles continuing to happen in Hungary.

2. Indexing Online

My little brother, gently prompted by my intuitive mother, convinced me to start indexing.

Initially I did batches of names out of duty to my brother (he's adorable, nearly impossible to say no to!) but one day a registry of Hungarian names popped up on my screen.

The Spirit swept over me and taught me that I was still able to help bring Hungarian souls to Christ—just on the other side of the veil!

For me, it was a miracle.

3. Setting Goals

I remember the first time I pulled out my list of goals after the mission. All my pre-mission life goals seemed unattainable with my new health condition.

After being discouraged for a time, I looked through my list again to find what I later called "horizontal goals"—goals that I could do while in bed.

I pursued several of these goals and set many new horizontal goals, from learning to play the harmonica to finishing reading *Jesus the Christ*.

> *Chelsea Jones*
> "I kept thinking, 'How am I going to feel in five years? Today it's awful, but in 2018, on August 15th, how am I going to feel?' And I would think about that. 'I'll probably be married. Hopefully I'll have a kid on the way or I'll be finishing school. Where do I want to be? These are the goals I want. What do I need to do to do them?' And I knew the only way I could achieve those goals was by staying in the gospel and staying in the Church. Even though 2013 was really hard and 2014 was really hard, in five years I'm not going to remember it. And the only way I knew for me personally I was able to do that is I had to stay with the gospel, I had to stay with the Church, and even if all my friends left me I still had that common core that I couldn't live without and couldn't change. So that's what helped me, having that perspective."

4. Returning to College

One of my pre-mission life goals was to graduate from college.

While attending classes would have been difficult with my body acting up and the constant doctor appointments, my dad encouraged me to take online classes from BYU Independent Study.

Not only was this an achievable horizontal goal, I realized that maybe I was capable of doing more pre-mission goals than I had previously thought possible.

5. Participating in a Service Mission

One day at church, a sister walked up to my mom and said, "Do you know that Destiny can serve an online mission?"

This unexpected question was an answer to my prayers. I was able to serve the Lord for nine months as an Indexing Support Church-service missionary. This was a mission I could do!

While many of you will feel that your mission is complete, some of you may feel (like I did) that you are supposed to serve a bit longer as a missionary.

If this is the case for you, I suggest reading an article I wrote in the August 2015 *Ensign,* "Catching the Vision: All Missions Bring Souls to Christ," about the wonderful variety of missions available for young single adults or going to www.lds.org/ycsm for more info. (I recommend calling their office directly!)

6. Teaching Mission Prep

As I became better at managing my health condition, I began studying at a community college while doing my online mission.

I was asked to teach mission prep on Sunday evenings at the nearby institute. At first I felt extremely underqualified. I felt I hadn't served long enough to learn all the lessons an 18-month or 2-year mission offers.

But teaching mission prep helped me realize that my enthusiasm for missionary work had not waned and that even my short mission had provided me with many experiences that could be valuable for my students.

7. Volunteering at the MTC

After successfully attending a semester of college near my home, I moved to Utah to attend Brigham Young University. I roomed with one of the sisters from my mission and hung out regularly with a group of fellow Hungarian RMs.

At first, I could hardly walk by the Provo MTC without feeling a rush of conflicting emotions. But after some time, I started volunteering weekly at the MTC and I found that it was healing to meet the next generations of missionaries headed out to Hungary.

8. Performing Temple Work

A Hungarian sister, Edit, who has prepared over 150,000 names for the temple (so far), asked me to take some of her names and do their work.

It was a joy to do the saving ordinances for these Hungarians!

The temple has continued to bless and heal me. Just this last year, I had the opportunity to be a temple worker. It was miraculous to be able to see how many Hungarian names came through the temple while I was there. Even though there are only a few thousand LDS Hungarians on this side of the veil, there are untold numbers of Hungarians having their work done on the other side!

Seek the Lord's Help in Finding Meaning

The activities I just mentioned are by no means a check-off list for you to complete. Nor do they guarantee healing.

I simply found that these activities gave *me* meaning during the years and helped me feel His love for me. Read the ideas of other early RMs below to see what helped them.

Ask the Lord to know how *He* would have you find meaning in your post-mission life and find ways to help others.

How did you find meaning after the mission?

Megan

"Since coming home I have tried to do my best to serve. I have had the opportunity to return to the MTC and serve as an interpreter during devotionals, Sunday church services, and other meetings. I have had the opportunity to serve in the temple as a patron and as an ordinance worker. I have had a stronger desire to serve my family and those around me. I'm so far from perfect, but Heavenly Father has helped me every step of the way to give me opportunities to love and serve my fellow men."

Kiana Lindmeir

"I found that I got really into family history. I had never done it before. But I got so into it, and I scanned thousands of documents that my great grandma had. I just fell in love with it. And it felt good because I was still doing missionary work, it was just a different kind. I went to the temple a lot."

Hunter

"I told myself 'I'm going to keep up on my studies, I'm still going to get up and study my Spanish every morning, do my other studies, and that way, I'll be ready to go back out. I won't have lost any of my study time.' But to be able to go back out, you have to get the okay from your doctor, and so we were just waiting on that forever, and I was just sitting at home. And a couple months had gone by and I still hadn't gotten the okay from my doctor. So that's when I was thought, 'If I do go back out, that would be awesome, but as of right now I need to either go back to school or I need to get a job and be productive, because I'm not doing anything.'"

Courtney Dickson
"When I came back I thought, 'I don't know how long I'm going to be here. I don't want to make everyone miserable. I want to enjoy this time.' In succession I went through every one of my family members and helped them in a way that I couldn't have done before. Every single one of them. My sister got her mission call, my brother came home from a mission, I got to be a temple worker while I was home, and I got to work at the family history center. My grandma got baptized while I was there. Not everyone has the chance to have their grandma get baptized when they come home. But I think the Lord does have purposes in it all and it is just our decision to see it or not. If you're looking for it, you'll find it."

Marissa Hedelius
"I realized during my time home that it was no accident that I was brought home at that specific time. I had a good friend who was struggling with his testimony, and I believe my coming home to spend time with him was a testimony to him of God's timing. I was also able to be there for my family as they struggled through some things as well. Being home made me realize that God was able to use me as His tool in touching the hearts of His children in Alaska or Utah because I was blessed to be at the right place at the right time. Rather than view that time as a trial now, I see it as a great blessing

to be able to help those people while I was home, and in return they helped me."

"No matter our circumstances, no matter our challenges or trials, there is something in each day to embrace and cherish. There is something in each day that can bring us gratitude and joy if only we will see and appreciate it."

—*President Dieter F. Uchtdorf*

HOW DO I NAVIGATE MY FIRST SUNDAY BACK?

My most immediate concern getting off the plane was what my ward would think. Will they welcome me back? What will I say when they ask why I'm home? The thought of Sunday was overwhelming and part of me really didn't want to go to church. (Who am I kidding? ALL of me didn't want to go.)

> *Chelsea Jones*
> "Sundays were my least favorite days, which was the first time that had ever happened in my life."

Nearly every early RM that I have met expressed the fear of coming back to church. Generally these fears fell under three categories:

1. What will everyone think of me?
2. What do I say when everyone asks why I'm home?
3. Will my ward accept me?

From what I have read and seen, here are some suggestions that will make your Sundays go as smoothly as possible:

1. Meet with your bishop IMMEDIATELY

As much as you may want to just hole up in your room for a few months, I recommend meeting with your bishop **immediately** to discuss:

- Should he announce that you're home and welcome you back to the ward? (This may be easier than having individual conversations with every member in the ward.)
- When will you both be able to meet regularly over the next few months? (I recommend *at least* weekly during the first month. You need that support system.)
- Would you be able to pass the sacrament or give a prayer? (This may help members accept you back in the ward more quickly.)
- When would be a good time to give a homecoming talk? (I didn't give mine for three months, which was perfect for me.)
- How can the ward council best support you during this time? (Do you need a friend, home teachers and visiting teachers, meals delivered, priesthood blessings, etc.?)
- Would you like a calling or a responsibility?
- Are you planning on returning to the mission or staying? (Now is probably not the time to delve into this discussion. Keep the conversation simple and surface level at the beginning.)

Some of the above suggestions for discussion topics with your bishop may not be appropriate if you came home for transgression reasons. However, meeting with your bishop is the vital first step of your repentance process and will help you move forward in faith. [See section called *For Those of You Who Came Home for Transgression Reasons* for more information.]

One of the benefits of letting your bishop announce that you're home that first Sunday is that people won't be surprised when you show up. Believe me, as someone who didn't tell anyone, this can be a very good thing. People who are surprised say things they don't mean to say or avoid contact altogether because they don't know what to say. The bishop welcoming you home will set an example to your fellow members and help them feel more comfortable around you. It's like pulling off a Band-Aid. Just get it over with rather than having to slowly take it off yourself over the next hundred conversations over the next few months.

While you may want to talk to your bishop about getting back out on your mission immediately, your first priority is to heal (whether physically, emotionally or spiritually). That will take time. Pray to the Lord to know if your mission is complete or if He has more service for you to do in a proselyting mission or as a young Church-service missionary. Your well-meaning family, bishop, and fellow ward members may give their opinions on whether you should stay or go, **but this decision is between you and the Lord.**

Here are two great quotes from early RMs; one who did return and one who did not.

Marissa Hedelius

"For anyone coming home early for a surgery like mine, I'd suggest you first counsel with your mission president to see his thoughts and impressions regarding your specific case. If he feels like your time to end your mission has come and the Spirit confirms that to you personally, then go home with your head held high and never discount the time you did serve and the people you did touch. God has a plan for you, and there is a reason you don't know, and maybe never will, that brought you home early. You are as honorable as an elder or sister that served the full 2 years or 18 months, in my mind. "If you do counsel with your mission president and, like in my case, agree that returning to your mission field is right, then stay focused on that while you're home and by all means, return! Don't let the fear of coming home early a second time keep you from returning like it almost did to me. Going back was so hard for me the second time because I knew just how hard constant rejection and waking up at 6:30 to -20 degrees was, but when I returned I felt a renewed energy for the work and excitement to be a missionary."

Chandler Crockett
"That was every second of my thinking for seven months: 'I just can't wait to go back to New York. I can't wait.' And then I found out that I couldn't. But before that happened, my stake president was pushing for me to go back. One of the General Authorities spoke at our stake conference, and my stake president called me up and had me meet him and said, 'This is Brother Crockett. He recently returned home from a mission early for health reasons, and he's looking to

go back.' And the Elder looked at me and said, 'That's great. If you go back, great. But if you don't, that's okay too, as long as you are doing what you need to be doing.'"

There is a third option that I did not initially realize I had when I came home: the young Church-service missionary program. You may fear that your only two options are to serve a proselyting mission or not serve a mission at all. That was how I felt, so I desperately tried to stay in the mission even when my health was failing.

I recommend prayerfully considering the option to become a young Church-service missionary. If you are worthy, you would be able to serve in the seminary and institute programs, on Temple Square, in a local non-profit organization, in an addiction recovery program, in a temple, or at your area's mission home (or a combination of several of these). Or, like me, you would perhaps be able to serve from your bed as a family history specialist.

My friend, Sister Richards, served as a young Church-service missionary in the Church Office Building. She was transferred to help with Disability Services, where I was working at the time, and we built an immediate friendship. I want to share a portion of her mission story in her own words:

> "I remember now the night of the mission president and wife coming over to our apartment and explaining that I would be released as a full-time missionary but would be able to do a service mission. He called my home stake

president, and after my stake president extended the calling of a service mission, I remember being quiet for the longest time before my stake president said, "Sister Richards?" Despite the emotion going on, when the service mission idea had been mentioned, I remember feeling spiritually good about transferring to a service mission. Interestingly enough, the previous month, my counselor had mentioned the idea of a service mission, which had sounded pretty cool but seemed off topic in that moment. It was probably the Spirit giving me a sort of heads-up and letting me know that this was right.

"I came to the service mission broken but have been able to be a little more repaired. This mission has been an opportunity to come to know the Savior more, feel of Him, and gain a greater appreciation for Him in a way that I hope can last for a lifetime."

She then shared a quote from President Henry B. Eyring's talk "Priesthood and Personal Prayer" that immediately resonated with me:

"It will not be the offices held or the time served that will be weighed in the balance with the Lord. We know this from the Lord's parable of the laborers in the vineyard, where the pay was the same regardless of how long they served or where. They will be rewarded for how they served."

Meeting with your bishop as soon as possible will not only help your first Sunday at home but will also help you be in a place where you can receive an answer from the Lord about whether to return to the mission field, serve as a young Church-service missionary, or serve in your ward at home.

2. Let Friends Know Beforehand

Your first Sunday will be awkward. The more you understand that, the better you'll navigate returning to your home ward or a YSA ward. That said, letting a few trusted friends know that you're home early before your first Sunday will help things go more smoothly.

Reach out to a few friends in a text or an email and tell them you're nervous about Sunday and would appreciate their support. You can ask them to sit with you or walk with you between classes (or even ward off anyone who may be too forward in their questions). Believe me, the more people who know you're back *before* Sunday, the less difficult it will be to get up the courage to go.

Some early RMs have had their parents post their return on a blog or in a mass email. Don't be afraid to ask readers for their support or to allow you some space for a while as you heal.

3. Practice What You'll Say

Even with all of your preparations, you will have members who come up and ask you questions. What happened? Why are you home? Are you going back out?

Practice what you'll say beforehand to help you feel more comfortable. These are a few "scripts" I came up with to help you know what to say.

"What happened?"

> *My health was acting up so badly in the mission, I had to come home. I'm needing some time to heal. Thanks for asking.*

"Why are you home?"

> *Yep, I'm home earlier than I planned, but I'm looking forward to serving in the ward the best that I can!* (I know this is technically not an answer to the question, but you do not have to explain why you're home if it makes you uncomfortable. This is also a possible response for those of you who come home for transgression reasons.)

"Are you going back out?"

> *I'm not sure what the Lord has planned for me. Coming home now certainly wasn't in my plan, but I'll serve the best I can while I'm here.*

You may have noticed that each of these responses are kind and positive but also close down any further questions. You do not need to go into detail. Your reasons for coming home early are extremely personal and, frankly, none of their business. But I have found that most members will be asking to show they care, and you can answer them in a way that is gentle but doesn't encourage probing.

You may find that some members won't know what to say and so they'll avoid you. You may need to be proactive and reach out to them to help ease the tension.

> *Chandler Crockett*
> "A lot of times, if I don't really know the person, I'll just say, 'I had some health problems I needed to come home to figure out.' Because if someone says, 'Why'd you come home?' and I say, 'I'm bipolar and had a psychotic breakdown,' they'll think, 'Whoa' and freak out a bit, because that's not something that they normally hear. So if I'm really comfortable with them I'll slowly explain it to them. Usually it's just, 'I came home for health reasons.'"

All that said, most early RMs do have a couple of stories about members saying something cruel, or asking very personal questions, or assuming that you did not pray enough or get enough priesthood blessings to stay in the mission. You do not have to say ANYTHING that you're uncomfortable with. Turn to your family and friends for support and leave the conversation. Recognize that one person's opinion does NOT represent an entire ward's opinion.

An early RM named Megan shared with me that her branch president was not understanding and said very hurtful things.

> "After considering leaving the Church for those brief moments, the covenants I had made in the temple came to my mind. I realized that this man was just a man and that I could not leave the Church just because I had been offended by him. I wanted to keep my temple covenants and I didn't want to leave the Church because of one person's lack of kindness towards me."

If your family, friends, and ward family are not being supportive, remember that the Lord is there for you and completely understands why you're home. Pray for strength to continue to go to church and partake of the sacrament. You **need** the enabling power of the Savior's Atonement to get through this.

4. Engage in the Ward

Once you have navigated your first Sunday home, do your best to engage in the ward.

Yes, you may have significant health problems, anxiety or depression, or be struggling with an addiction. But talk with your bishop to see how you can serve to the best of your ability.

My health was shot after the mission. There was no way I could have done a traditional calling for the first few months. Thankfully, my brother got me involved in indexing and later on I served an online mission.

Get creative and brainstorm with your bishop. Maybe there is a calling you can do from home or online. Maybe you can home or visit teach the members who can only be reached by mail. Maybe you can have a small responsibility until you are able to receive an official calling. Do everything you can to stay connected with your ward. Feeling needed does wonders for healing.

———

How did you navigate your first Sunday home?

Micaela Rice
"My biggest fear coming home was that people would think I failed or they wouldn't understand my injury and why I couldn't have stayed out there. I think I just didn't want to disappoint anyone, when, really, I was the only one disappointed with myself. I feel like that is one of the biggest ways Satan works on early RMs. He makes you believe you failed and that no one will accept your service, but in all reality I have come across only a handful that haven't, and the majority of people have been so loving and accepting."

Christie Hansen
"I completely understood how people go inactive when they came home early, with the feelings they are dealing with themselves, let alone how everyone else treats them. I understood it; I refused to be

113

one of those people though. I had just spent the last few months of my life preaching about the gospel. There was no way I was going to let go of what had been my strength for so long, what had gotten me through so much, and what I had just watched change people's lives in ways they could not imagine. I could not ever in my life imagine leaving what had meant so much to me that I was ready to give up a year and a half of my life to help others find it."

Courtney Dickson
"It definitely was not easy. I tell people it was easier to serve a mission than it was to come home from one. I just had learn to deal with people, not worrying about what people thought of me."

Hunter Jones
"I think early returned missionaries need to understand that it's always going to be weird, but you don't have to justify yourself to anybody. It's your personal situation, and if that does get brought up, you can tell people what happened but then you don't have to explain anything to anybody.

"I came home for medical reasons, and it got twisted around to I was coming home because I was doing something wrong. Nobody wants to go to church and feel unwelcome and judged the whole time, even though you are there for you. I don't remember anything specific that made me just have a change of mind and just go and not care, but you know, that's just what I did. I thought, 'People can think whatever they want. I'm just going to go to church.'"

Jenny Rollins

"Give people the benefit of the doubt. It will be easy to find reasons to be offended by people who may really care about you but might not know how to react to your situation. Focus on the people who are rooting for you and be forgiving of those who pass judgment" ("*Dealing with Coming Home Early*," July 2016 Ensign).

"Something else that I wish I would have known before is that sometimes if you give people a specific way to help you and let them do it, it makes them feel included. When you don't actually give them anything to do, then you feel like you're kind of distancing yourself and they feel like they're being ostracized a little bit. So you can say, 'Hey, you know, I know that my mom is really stressed about this if you could bring dinner over one night, that would be awesome.' Or 'If you can come over and play a board game with me and distract me [from the pain] for a little bit, that would be awesome.' Or 'If you want to get together and do companionship scripture study so I can feel like I'm still keeping that up, that would be great.' Even if you can't figure out ways for them to serve you, you can always figure out ways for them to help the people that are serving you."

Amy Van Heel

"It was wonderful to see my family again and so hard to be released. Everyone was welcoming and kind. They didn't ask too many questions and when I told them I came home early, they didn't judge me like I thought they would."

Megan

"When I arrived home, it felt like a huge weight was lifted off of my shoulders. But I also had doubts several times after getting home that maybe I had made the wrong decision or that maybe it was all in my head. I was also worried about what other people would think of me. Most people just didn't say anything and just treated me normally. It was almost like they pretended I had never even left on a mission. I guess this helped me because I was able to avoid the awkward conversations of having to explain everything, but at the same time, I guess I kind of still felt embarrassed because I never did get the chance to explain. Eventually those feelings of embarrassment passed and I began to feel comfortable around people again."

Chelsea Jones

"One thing that I definitely can recommend to a missionary who returns home early, no matter what the reason is, either anxiety or disobedience, either before or during the mission, the fact that you are coming home to fix whatever is going on, or because you put in the amount of work that you are able to handle and then you need to come home and finish your work there, it doesn't matter what anyone else thinks. And I know you can say that, but whether you actually believe it is a completely different thing. It took me a long, long time—longer than I'd like to admit—to finally understand that. The only person who matters is the One who actually knows your story, probably better than you do."

Chandler Crockett

"Everyone was very supportive. The Sunday after I got home, while I was in the hospital, they announced in church that I had come home for some health reasons. That was all they said. But the ward, they were really good, no one asked me, 'Hey, why'd you come home?' I don't think a single person asked me that. Just, 'How are you doing? Are you okay?' They were really respectful. I gave my homecoming talk a year after I came home, and I opened up and told them what happened."

Britt Barlow

"I did go back my first Sunday, and everyone was really happy to see me. And they asked, 'Oh, what happened?' I just told them, 'I'm really sick.' The biggest thing I got was, 'You don't look sick.' And I said, 'It's because I'm wearing makeup and I'm pretending to be fine.' I think the huge thing when you come home is to not be offended, because they're not trying to offend you. They care about you. So they'd say, 'What happened?' and I'd explain it to them, and they were really nice about it. And something I learned to do is when they'd say, 'Oh, are you feeling well enough to go back out?' I'd tell them the truth. I'd say, 'I feel terrible, and I don't know if I *can* go back out or if I'm going to.' And then they'd say, 'Oh, okay!' So then they started asking me how I was doing and how I was feeling, rather than, 'When are you going back out?'"

"If we are serious about our discipleship, Jesus will eventually request each of us to do those very things which are most difficult for us to do."

—*Elder Neal A. Maxwell*

WILL I EVER FEEL OKAY ABOUT THIS?

It hurt so badly to think about my mission.

In my mind, I had failed the Lord *and* failed the Hungarians I 'would have' taught if I stayed. I tried to forget my mission and sometimes wished I had never gone in the first place. What made me even more sad was that, unlike my parents who loved telling us about their missions, I didn't want to tell my future kids about my mission because it would hurt too badly and they would think I failed as well. I wondered when (if) I would ever tell them about what 'really' happened on my mission.

To me, there was no possible way to heal after my mission, so the only option was to forget/ignore it as much as possible. I would jump back and forth between wanting to hop a flight and try to 'fix' what I thought I had messed up over there and being absolutely terrified at the thought of going back. Eventually I decided that going back to visit my mission was simply out of the question—it would hurt way too much.

The thing was ... I didn't understand the Atonement at all.

Four years after my mission and a whole lot of mini steps forward in my progress (so mini that I couldn't really tell if I had improved or not) I had the opportunity to visit Hungary again. I think the Lord helped me not really think about it too much until I got there. It was a spur-of-the-moment trip, and I hopped the bus to Budapest before I had really thought it through. On my second day in the country, it suddenly hit me that I was feeling no pain—I was only feeling blissful joy to be there in Budapest meeting with my Hungarian brothers and sisters.

That realization blew me away.

Wait a second. Wasn't it my lot in life to *always* feel pain about my mission? Instead, I was in Hungary and feeling only joy. I realized that after four long years, I had finally reached a point in my healing I never imagined possible.

On that incredible day, I wrote in my journal:

> [22 June 2013]
> *I am sitting in Hungary, reading my scriptures, and in a good place spiritually in my life. What a blessing I didn't come to Hungary earlier!*
>
> *Wow, what a **miracle** to be here in Hungary and be **so happy**—there has been almost no sadness, regret, or anger while here. I think coming [here] is one of the final steps of the healing process in regards to my mission. Wow, it's almost surreal. ... I've come so far; He has helped me heal so much. Something I thought would NEVER be possible!*
>
> [23 June 2013]
> *Wow, it has been a hard, long four years, but I **know** this is my mission. I was supposed to come here. I remember thinking, "Was I supposed to come on my mission?"... Now I know that I was supposed to come because of everything that*

happened today. This was a challenge that came not because I wasn't supposed to go, but maybe because I was supposed to learn a ton. ... If I don't see [Hungary] again, I'm so glad I came back at <u>this</u> time! I'm so blessed—my heart is settled—this was huge closure for me!

[25 June 2013]
Like Enos, I think, "Lord, how is this done?" How is my guilt gone, how is my regret gone?

*It wasn't going back to visit my mission that healed me—going back just highlighted the healing that the Lord had been quietly doing over the years. It was only there [in Hungary], when emotional triggers are going off, memories are coming back and I'm meeting the people I left, that I could **know** His atoning power and capacity to <u>heal</u> the seemingly eternal pain that we experience in life.*

Let me reemphasize one thing that I wrote back then.

"It wasn't going back to visit my mission that healed me—going back just highlighted the healing that the Lord had been quietly doing over the years." The Lord, in His patience and grace, was giving me the opportunity over the four years to take steps in my progress, to heal very painful wounds. And to be honest, even just last week, I realized that He had led me to take another huge step in my healing process in regards to my mission.

He is consistently finding ways to take this experience and use if for good.

Remember the Lord's warning to Peter about how he would deny Him three times? Prior to making that prophesy, the Lord says, "Simon, Simon, behold, Satan hath desired to have you, that he may sift you as wheat: But I have prayed for thee, that thy faith fail not: and **when** thou art converted, strengthen thy brethren." Peter, not knowing the future, optimistically declares, "Lord, I am ready to go with thee, both into prison, and to death" (Luke 22:31–33).

When I read this, a few things stand out to me. First of all, I love Peter's enthusiasm to give the Lord his heart. I think many of us felt that kind of confidence as we left for our missions.

The second thing that stands out to me is that the Lord says, "*when* thou art converted.*" It's like He's telling Peter that, yes, he will definitely stumble and fall, but he can make it through this. *When* implies a future success if he hangs in there.

The last thing to stand out was that the Lord also tells Peter that after he is converted (or makes it through the healing process), "strengthen thy brethren." This hit me hard because I realized that my Heavenly Father always uses hard experiences for good—for the good of the person going through the experience ... and for others nearby as well. My mom shared this verse with me recently:

Doctrine and Covenants 98:3

*Therefore, he giveth this promise unto you, with an immutable covenant that they shall be fulfilled: and **ALL things wherewith you have been afflicted** shall work together for your good and to my name's glory, saith the Lord.*

I realized that He has used my afflictions to help me grow and that He had helped me heal to this point so that I could "strengthen" others who are going through this experience today. And I have no doubt that, if you let Him, He will help you do the same.

Micaela Rice
"My mom was the one who actually started my blog while I was on my mission, and when I came home she kept encouraging me to continue it and to share my experience of coming home. It took me a month before I wrote about my story and then another month for me to decide to keep updating it. Now I just write whenever I am having feelings about my mission and coming home early."

So, whether you feel it is time to strengthen others now or if, like me, it takes a few years before you feel it is time to help others, remember that the Lord can help you use this experience for your good and for the good of others if you let Him!

He knew this would happen, and He planned for it.

Orson F. Whitney
"No pain that we suffer, no trial that we experience is wasted. It ministers to our education, to the development of such qualities as patience, faith, fortitude, and humility. All that we suffer and all that we endure, especially when we endure it patiently, builds up our characters, purifies our hearts, expands our souls, and makes us more tender and charitable, more worthy to be called the children of God."

What a blessing it is that even our hardest/weakest moments can be utilized for some bigger plan! What a miracle it is that He can understand and take upon Him our pain! What a joy it is to know that He **knew** this would happen and prepared "a way for [us] that [we] may accomplish the thing which he commandeth [us]" (1 Ne. 3:7).

In one of my lowest moments, I cried to the Lord, "If You knew I was going to fall on my face, why did you let me go on a mission? Why did you let this happen to me?"

I had forgotten that this is the Lord that we're talking about. He has a way prepared for you and I, no matter the reason we came home from the mission early. Think about the lost 116 pages of the Book of Mormon. The Lord knew that Martin Harris and Joseph Smith, in their human weakness, would slip up, and so He had Mormon prepare a backup plan 1,630 years ago by including both Lehi's and Nephi's words in the Book of Mormon. And Mormon, following the Spirit's guidance, says, "And now, I do not know all things; but the Lord knoweth all things which are to come; wherefore, he worketh in me to do according to his will" (Words of Mormon 1:7).

The point Mormon is sharing with us is that if your heart is willing and humble, the Lord "worketh in [you] to do according to his will"—no matter the reason you came home. As you navigate the ups and downs that come with this kind of experience, remember in the back of your mind that the Lord can use this to help others.

You can do it!

I can only imagine what you are feeling right now.

For years, everything was a blur and I struggled to make sense out of something that seemed like such a waste. But (thankfully) He saw a bigger purpose and gave me this opportunity to grow. It may take you years, like it took me, to see the blessings and lessons learned from this experience. But you can do this! Hang on to the gospel until you get your feet under you again! Surround yourself with people who know your heart and your desire to grow! All of us early-returned missionaries struggle along the way and bump around to find meaning in this kind of traumatic experience, BUT so many survive and witness the miracle of God's grace!

> *Brigham Young*
> If members of the Church had the eternities in full vision before their minds, he said, "there is not a trial which the

Saints are called to pass through that they would not realize and acknowledge to be their greatest blessing."

I am praying for you. You have parents, mission presidents, bishops, and/or friends praying for you. If you feel alone and do not have any support system, reach out to me at yarbro.destiny@gmail.com and I'll hook you up with an early-returned missionary who can help mentor you through this coming-home process.

When you question yourself from the inside out and are hard on yourself, remember that **no** missionary leaves home planning on coming home early. We all had a genuine desire to serve a mission, no matter what happened after that point. Hold to that and remember that deep down inside, **you desire good.**

Decide today to make this experience a stepping stone in the right direction. Make this a step forward, not a step backward. Remember that Heavenly Father is **eager** to help you navigate this!

———

If you could go back to your flight home and tell your past self something, what would you say?

Britt Barlow
"Have the mentality that it's okay if it's hard. It might take a while, but it's going to be okay. And you may not *know* how it's going to be okay or how it can possibly be worked out for your good, but

just have some tiny particle of faith that somehow God can make it work out in the long run."

Christie Hansen
"If I could give any advice it would be learn from it. You can't change what happened, but you can learn from it and have it help you shape your future. Though you may not understand what is going on, Heavenly Father does and He sees the big picture, so go along with Him and you will discover a life you never imagined."

Parker Tyler
"Just keep going, just keep trying, because you're guaranteed to fail if you stop. And even if you feel like a failure at times, you're not going to fail because the Lord is on your side."

Kiana Lindmeir
"I think I was so uncertain of what was going to happen and so disappointed in myself. If I could go back, I'd tell myself, 'Kiana, you are incredible. You're amazing. You've done *great* work. And it's okay to be home. You're not a failure.' I just would go back and say, 'You're doing awesome' and just let myself know that it was okay because it *was* hard."

Micaela Rice
"I would say to give yourself time to heal. Don't rush the process. It takes time. I have been home for eight months, and I am still trying to heal. Let this trial run its course. As hard as it is to be home early when it wasn't in your plan, it was in Heavenly Father's plan and

He has given you this time to either spend with your family, learn something new, or call you to a new responsibility."

Lindsay Farnworth
"In that moment I wish someone would have given me a huge long hug and expressed that they knew everything was not okay right now but that it would be someday. I wish I would have been reassured that this wasn't something that I had control over, but it was a part of God's plan for me. I would have told myself that I was at a crossroad. I could choose to become bitter and lose my testimony, or I could choose to cling to my testimony and allow God to change my life. I would have told myself that I was about to go through some of the hardest days I had ever experienced but that those days would be how I would come to build a solid relationship with my Savior and Father in Heaven.

"I would have told myself that my focus now needs to be on learning how to take care of myself and to work to become healthy. It may not seem like it, but that is a worthy purpose. I would have reminded myself of the line in my call that said, 'It is anticipated that you will serve for a period of 18 months.' I would point out that never meant that I would serve 18 months and reassure myself that there was no pressure to go back out. The most important expectations were God's expectations for me, and my honorable release meant my two-month mission was perfect for my life!"

Darcy Lethco

"I learned that nobody around you knows exactly what you're feeling or going through, but He does."

Madison Stevenson

"Stay close to God and do what He asks, and as you do that, your heart will soften and you will understand that everything happens for a reason. God is on your side. He loves you so much that He is willing to push you to your limit so you can return to Him!"

Amy Van Heel

"While you feel broken, know that it is okay to go through a hard time. You don't have to be perfect, happy, and okay right now. Don't be afraid to get help. Please, please don't dwell on the problem. Don't think people are judging you, and if they do, well, you don't need them in your life. They just don't understand what you are going through. They can't comprehend it because they've never been in your shoes. When we see a baby fall down, do we get mad at them? NO! We are excited to see them trying to learn, to grow and to become better. That is how Heavenly Father is with us, His children. Remember it is about progress, not perfection."

Marissa Hedelius

"Go home with your head held high and never discount the time you did serve and the people you did touch. God has a plan for you, and there is a reason you don't know, and maybe never will, that brought you home early. Gratefully, His will for me was to return to Alaska, but I know that if His will was for me to stay, that would make His power no less remarkable in my life."

Chandler Crockett

"This is something my stake president told me when I found out I couldn't go back to New York, and I was just stressing about mission, mission, mission. He said, 'You know, a mission is just a very small fraction of your life. Now we're looking at exaltation. We're looking at your future.' Your mission is just tiny. I don't want to say insignificant, but your mission does not determine everything. It's just a small thing. It's not everything."

Megan

"Don't give up! Your life is so worth living! There is a place for you! You are needed! You are wanted! Don't worry about what other people say that may be judgmental or unkind. You are worth so much in the eyes of Heavenly Father. It may take time to figure out what you are supposed to be doing at this time in your life, but the revelation and guidance WILL come. Maybe you will be prompted and able to go back on a full-time mission or maybe you won't. Either way, there are so many opportunities to serve. You can strengthen those around you right where you stand. You can bloom where you are planted."

Jenny Rollins

"It is all going to work out. Not only is it going to be okay, but it is going to be better. I'm living proof that God definitely has a plan and I can't predict it. And I don't have to. I can trust Him and I can do the very best that I can and He is going to guide me and even though He may guide me through ways that are really, really painful and that I didn't expect, I'm going to be better off for it and I'm going to help a lot of people. Honestly, being a full-time missionary is one of the most incredible things you can do; it's also not THE most incredible thing that you can do. I'd remind myself that I'm still capable of doing amazing things."

Courtney Dickson

"It's not going to be easy. I'm sorry you have to go through this, 'cause it stinks. But there's purpose in your suffering, and the Lord trusts you with this learning experience. And that's why He's placed it in your life, because there'll be things you learn through this process and suffering experience that in the future you're going to be sitting across from someone you're only able to help because of the hard things you've gone through. And if you accept that and seek for that in your life, the Lord will give you opportunity after opportunity after opportunity to help people, help His children.

"Don't try to figure out the purpose of your life all in one sitting. It's not going to happen! I'm still figuring it out. But health issues I think are really hard. I found that when Satan can't affect you spiritually or emotionally, he gets at you physically, because when you're physically down, then your spirit goes down and your emotions go down. But it's not a punishment from Heavenly Father that you're sick. Sometimes it's a blessing. I think that the Lord has a purpose in it all. Read your patriarchal blessing. Find meaning. Don't give up. Listen to Elder Holland's quote that says, 'Don't Give Up' (See "An High Priest of Good Things to Come")."

Ryan Freeman

"Most missionaries would say that coming home from a mission is full of excitement. Unfortunately, when you are an early-returned missionary, that is often not the case. In fact, my return home was full of dread. I think many people have this idyllic image of a homecoming, a celebration of the missionary's service. Sometimes I see pictures that remind me of a birthday party, which is fitting because there is a newness to the whole situation. But in my case, I felt like my return was more of a funeral. Gone were my hopes of being a successful missionary and successful son.

"As time went by, I realized how wrong my view of the situation was. My return absolutely deserved celebration and excitement. I had learned a lot, and perhaps more important, I had tried. Maybe some people wouldn't understand, but I did. And there were many who were able to bear my burdens instead of gossiping about them.

"Never until that time had my strengths and weaknesses, my gifts and abilities, my hopes and aspirations been so clear. There was so much noise when I returned. Whether from those around me or from my own head. It was only when I learned to be mindful and meditative that I found peace in the still and small.

"One of the last comments made to me before leaving was from a missionary. He said, 'Whatever happens, don't let Satan win.' That worry consumed me. Was I simply letting Satan win? What if I couldn't return, was I some kind of minion? In the end, I realized that some people choose to see life as a series of struggles with demons, but I prefer to take the example of Jacob's wrestle with an angel (see Genesis 32). We all are called upon to wrestle with the divine, and Jacob refuses to let go until he is blessed. Coming home when I did was a blessing, and I absolutely believe it brought me closer to God."

"It is extremely important for you to believe in yourselves not only for what you are now but for what you have the power to become. Trust in the Lord as He leads you along. He has things for you to do that you won't know about now but that will unfold later. If you stay close to Him, You will have some great adventures. ... The Lord will unfold your future bit by bit."

—*Elder Neal A. Maxwell*

AFTERWORD FROM DESTINY

I am moving in a couple of weeks and have been cleaning out my clothes for my one last stop to Deseret Industries before I go. I pulled out my mission suit coat and tried to lay it in the give-away pile. It's old and frayed and I have hardly worn it since getting back, but I just couldn't do it. I started to cry as I put the jacket in my small to-keep pile.

Seeing that jacket reminded me of the first time I put on one of my mission outfits in 2009. I was standing with my mom in our living room, and my dad walked in from work and got teary as he told me he was so happy for me. The three of us hugged and cried with joy together.

Holding my jacket today, I cried because it was a hard memory for me. After all, we had no clue at the time what was coming in the way of my mission. I also cried because so much has happened since my mission and I find myself in awe that I could emotionally handle writing this book over the last few years.

My point is, I imagine that I will still have moments when I cry because of how my mission turned out. It is normal to mourn sometimes, no matter how long it's been. As much as I have healed so far, I still have days when I wish I could have just served a year-and-a-half–long mission and come home to a family celebration in the airport.

Let yourself hurt and let yourself laugh as you process this experience.

If you would have asked me three years ago if I'd ever feel okay about my mission, I would have told you "NO." I truly thought that healing would never come in this life. And for some of you, that may be true. But we must trust in His ability to make all things right in the end.

We must trust that *healing will come.*

Seven Years

[20 February 2016]
In five days it will have been seven years since I walked into the MTC. In a way, I guess my time since the mission has been my seven years of famine and my seven years of plenty (Gen. 41: 29–30). I have "seen [my] weakness" (Ether 12:37) but have also learned that "[His] grace is sufficient" (2 Cor. 12:9). I have felt so lost and alone, but I have also seen the most amazing "tender mercies of the Lord" (1 Ne. 1:20). I have seen the enabling and forgiving powers of Jesus Christ's Atonement "make weak things become strong" in my life (Ether 12:27). He has been with me every step of the way and I know that He will be there for you.

... Now What?

"Simon ... I have prayed for thee, that thy faith fail not: and when thou art converted, strengthen thy brethren (Luke 22:31, 32).

When the time comes, you will have the opportunity to share your experience with someone else who has returned from the mission early. The Lord will lead them to you because you will be able to give them encouragement from a fellow early RM. You will be able to share what you learned, what you wish you would have known when you were flying home on the plane, and how the Lord has helped you heal step-by-step.

Or perhaps, like other early RMs, you will start websites, blogs, podcasts, webinars, or books. [See **Resources** on earlyRM.com for other sources of help.]

I mention helping others not to add pressure but to add hope to your current situation.

The Lord knows what you are going through and no doubt already has a plan in place for you to help others through your experiences. The opportunity to share may happen soon or, like me, it may happen seven years from now.

Until then—and when you are ready—write me an email at yarbro.destiny@gmail.com.

Feel free to share your experience. Consider sharing what your greatest fears are and what tender mercies you have seen. Consider sharing what you are learning about the Savior and His Atonement and what you wish you would have known before you came home.

Most importantly, though, feel free to ask ANY questions you may have. I may not have the answers, but after having so many conversations with early RMs, I hope we can at least have an uplifting discussion together.

Hold to the faith, my friends.
"Doubt not, fear not" (Doctrine and Covenants 6:36).

Destiny Yarbro
20 February 2016
yarbro.destiny@gmail.com

"Sometimes we consider changes in our plans
as missteps on our journey.
Think of them more as first steps to
being 'on the Lord's errand.'"

—Elder Ronald A. Rasband

"Jesus Christ has overcome the world. And because of Him, because of His infinite Atonement, we all have great cause to trust, knowing that ultimately all will be well."

—*Sister Bonnie H. Cordon*

SHORT GUIDES FOR PARENTS, BISHOPS / STAKE PRESIDENTS, MISSION PRESIDENTS, AND WARD COUNCILS

After reading and listening to the challenges of and lessons learned by over a thousand early RMs, I have come to realize more than ever that **you are CRITICAL to an early RM's success**.

While it is ultimately their decision to stay active, I must be bold in saying that you can either make or break a missionary. Your impact on how they view their mission will be felt for the rest of their lives. (I am not just saying that. I have read multiple stories about the impact a mission president or a family member had on their son or daughter's return decades ago.)

For better or for worse, your initial reaction does make a difference.

That being said, if you are reading this book, chances are that you are handling it better than you think.

I have purposefully chosen to write only a small amount of content for each of you. Ideally, a parent would be able to glance through this guide on their way to the airport. A bishop would be able to read through this guide to support parents and missionaries immediately after receiving the call that a missionary is coming home. A ward council would be able to read through this guide before a missionary's first Sunday back. Perhaps even a mission president would be able to glance through this guide before telling a missionary they are going home.

These are not check-off lists or one-size-fits-all guides, but simply suggestions gathered from many, *many* conversations with early RMs.

When a missionary learns that they will be coming home earlier than anticipated, most will feel the stigma and pressure immediately. You have the opportunity to be their support system.

Help them heal and turn to the Lord

Everything else can stay on hold for a while.

Before we proceed to the one-page guides, I want to give you a glimpse into the impact you can have on a missionary. These are quotes from early RMs in a BYU study conducted in part by Ryan Freeman (also an early RM). Positive experiences are in normal print while negative experiences are in italics.

PARENTS

"They were totally supportive! Met me at the airport with a full welcome home. Told me they were proud and that anxiety like I had is a medical condition, not a spiritual condition. Helped me get a job. I am doing much better now."

"I could tell they were concerned and cared about me. They shared with me scriptures and stories from Church history about others whose lives did not go as planned and how it became a positive thing in their lives in the future if they did not become bitter towards it."

"My parents were my rock. I would not have been able to make it through the constant criticism [from others] without their love and support."

"My parents ... were embarrassed because I had come home early without a diagnosis. My mom's direct words after hearing from the doctor that I needed knee surgery were, 'Wow, so glad something is really wrong! I am not sure what I would have done if they had not found the crack.'"

"I am the oldest of four brothers. My mother asked me one day, once it was decided that I wouldn't be returning, if I could please talk to each of them and explain to them that coming home early from a mission is not okay. It was devastating to me. I felt disappointed in myself already and then felt as though I had let down my family too. This was very difficult to work through."

BISHOPS and STAKE PRESIDENTS

"He congratulated me and told me that I should hold my head high and that I served an honorable mission. He said that I should always remain faithful, remember the work I did out in the field, and that now I should start planning my future."

"He continued to meet with me weekly and gave me a temporary calling in the priests quorum and as a ward missionary. I appreciated feeling like I was useful to some degree."

149

"[He] hasn't approached, called, or even really asked how I'm doing. I'm struggling and having a hard time. Depressed."

"I wish he would not have treated me like coming home [for depression] was a bad thing. I wish he wouldn't have hidden me from the young men and members of the ward. I would have loved to report on my mission. I had a lot of great experiences."

"No counsel from my bishop. He viewed my returning home early as a weakness, and he didn't want the 'young men in the ward to think that it was okay to return home early from their missions.'"

MISSION PRESIDENTS

"[My mission president] was very supportive and helpful. I think he was my biggest supporter."

"His compassion made all the difference in how I felt about my mission."

"He was a huge support through the whole process. He always listened, and he gave me blessings and helped when needed. He told me that they often prayed for me by name."

"I wish my mission president understood better what depression is. My mission president told me to pray harder. It's hard to be seen as a weak or less faithful as a missionary when I was working as hard as I possibly could—more than was probably healthy for me. My mission

president was a good man and generally compassionate, but he did not understand depression as an illness."

"I felt like a burden to everyone. I felt like I was one more problem they wanted to hurry and get resolved."

"My mission president's wife did make me feel guilty about needing to go to the doctor because of the cost."

"I was told, despite the fact that I was an exceptionally obedient and disciplined missionary, that I needed more faith. I was told to pray and read my scriptures (as if I wasn't already)."

HOW THE STIGMA AFFECTS MISSIONARIES

"To this day I'm still left wondering if my offering was acceptable to the Lord."

"When I was on my mission, I felt like I let the Lord down. I couldn't understand why I was not healed from the blessing that promised I would if I had enough faith. I really felt like I had a lot of faith, and more than anything, I wanted to be cured and stay on my mission. I wish I could have talked to someone about the feelings I was having."

"Those who have served missions with no medical problems don't understand how the missionary feels."

"I wish I wouldn't have felt so alone on my return. Coming home is hard enough, but coming home early was awful, awkward, and full of misunderstandings."

"It was an awful experience that is hard to recover from. I just want to get on with my life and forget it ever happened."

"When I was sent home the second time, I made all of my problems internal. I thought, "If I can't even handle a mission, how am I going to handle having a job and kids and a future?""

"It was hard to feel like I was one of those missionaries who couldn't finish. Still today, nearly three years later, I struggle with thoughts of inadequacy and guilt."

"I had never heard of a missionary getting sick while in the mission field. It would have been very helpful to have someone pick up the phone and tell me I was not the first person to leave the mission field early to illness."

"Just [have] compassion, no judgments. It was hard enough to go home as it was."

Short Guide for Parents

If I could tell you one thing:

Your missionaries will feel pressure from everyone around them. Counselors, friends, ward members, and bishops will ask questions and give advice. For now, your job is to gently support and protect your missionary until they are ready to stand on their own again. They do not need more pressure; they need unconditional love.

1. Tell your missionary immediately how much you love them and are proud of them.

Be proud of their willingness to serve the Lord. Be proud of the time they *did* serve. If they came home for transgression reasons, coming home is the first step forward and can be applauded.

2. Ask your missionary what they would prefer at the airport.

Some early-returned missionaries were grateful to return home to a full traditional welcome in the airport with balloons, posters, and extended family. Other missionaries were grateful to get off the plane and see just their parents there. Pray for sensitivity.

3. Let your missionary lead out when processing.

No matter what the technical reason is for coming home, a missionary may not feel ready to share about their experience for some time. Let them process on their own timetable. Pray to know when to be a listening ear and when to be a happy distraction. Recognize that they may need someone else besides you to process with, maybe even a fellow early RM.

4. Make healing the top priority of both you and your missionary.

Your number one priority must be to help them heal physically, emotionally, and spiritually. This experience may be more traumatic for them than you think, and healing will take time. Your missionary may experience unexpected emotional triggers for years afterward. Set questions related to returning to the mission or returning to college aside for a time. When it's time to address going back out, allow the missionary to receive their own answer from the Lord. Encourage those around your missionary to accept their answer fully.

5. Help them feel hope.

An early RM will most likely feel confused and lost upon their return home. Help them notice tender mercies every day. Help them find meaningful ways to serve. Help them laugh. (My family put on *I Love Lucy* every day to give me regular opportunities to smile.) Help them set post-mission goals rather than dwell on pre-mission goals. Help them identify successes. When it is appropriate, help them feel capable and ready to progress in their lives.

Short Guide for Bishops and Stake Presidents

If I could tell you one thing:

Your ward or stake will often follow your example in how you welcome an early RM.

1. Meet with the missionary's parents *before* the missionary returns.

Besides a quick phone call from the mission president (and sometimes not even that), parents will know very little about how to support an early RM. Even if you are not sure about what to do either, meeting with them prior to the missionary's return shows your support and a willingness to work directly with them during this time. While the parents will meet many of the needs of their missionary, they may need the ward to help meet their own needs. Consider bringing the Short Guide for Parents with you to your first visit. If you hear a missionary is coming home, do not assume that the mission president has called the parents directly and do your best to alert them and support them through the process. There have been times when parents have not found out about their missionary's return until last minute because priesthood leaders have assumed others have informed the parents.

2. Meet with the missionary as soon as possible.

It is absolutely vital that you meet with the missionary immediately upon their return and regularly over the next few months (at least). Similar to a convert, this missionary needs "a friend, a responsibility, and nurturing with 'the good word of God'" (Gordon B. Hinckley, "Converts and Young Men," May 1997 *Ensign*). Do not make assumptions regarding the reason a missionary came home. Misunderstandings can be devastating. If a missionary came home for transgression, prayerfully consider treating their return as their first step to repentance.

Consider discussing some of the following questions in your first meeting:

- When will you be able to meet regularly over the next few months? (I recommend *at least* weekly during the first month. Trust grows with experience.)
- Should you announce that they are home and formally welcome them back to the ward? (This may be easier for the missionary than individual conversations with every member in the ward over the following few months.)
- If appropriate, would they like to pass the sacrament or give the closing prayer? (This can help members accept an early RM back into the ward more quickly.)
- When would be a good time for them to give a talk in church? (Most returned missionaries are asked to give a talk. This invitation is often neglected in the case of early RMs. Be aware that some might not feel emotionally ready, but giving them the opportunity can help them feel accepted.)

- How can the ward council best support them during this time? (Do they need a friend, home teachers and/or visiting teachers, meals delivered, priesthood blessings, etc.?)
- If appropriate, would they like a calling or a responsibility?

3. Realize that it may or may not be the Lord's will for a missionary to return to the field.

While you may have to ask whether a missionary is considering returning to the mission or not, do not add pressure. This is an extremely personal decision between the missionary and the Lord. Allow the missionary to receive their own revelation on the matter.

4. In the case of transgression:

There is no one reason why a missionary came home early, especially for transgression reasons. Prayerfully seek to know whether your particular missionary returned for an addiction they could not overcome, confession of a sin committed prior to the mission, not stopping a companion's behavior, or willful rebellion. While you'll approach each reason differently, proceed with love for all.

Bishops now have access to a "Ministering Resource" on helping early-returned missionaries at providentliving.lds.org.

Short Guide for Mission Presidents

Mission presidents are some of the few that have information directly from the Church to help you navigate missionaries' early return. While this is not an official guide below, it is a list of suggestions stemming from many conversations with early RMs.

If I could tell you one thing:

You set the tone for how the missionary views their mission. If you help them understand that a mission is not about length but a desire to serve, they will have a desire to seek for Heavenly Father's help as they navigate this trial.

1. Proceed with the assumption that the missionary has done their best.

I would venture a guess that no missionary has ever left for his mission saying, "See you in two months, Mom!" Missionaries do not plan on returning home early. Trust that most have tried to stay in the mission as long as they could (or should). When appropriate, talk with them about their strengths and their contribution to the mission. They will hold onto what you say in the hard times ahead.

2. Recognize that the missionary may feel a lot of fear and/or be traumatized.

Many early RMs fear that they have failed the Lord. Reassuring a missionary that missions come in all types and lengths can help them feel less anxiety about returning. Encourage them to be kind to themselves and to allow themselves to heal over the months and years ahead.

3. Give the missionary possible next steps to consider.

Whatever the reason for sending a missionary home early, gently remind them that there are many ways to serve the Lord. Encourage them to reach out to their bishops immediately and ask for a calling/responsibility. There may be some who feel that their mission is not over. Tell all worthy missionaries returning about the young Church-service missionary program [lds.org/ycsm]. Some missionaries can begin their new service mission within hours of returning.

4. Give as much information to the parents as possible.

Too many parents I have spoken with have been absolutely clueless that their child was coming home until last minute because a mission office did not contact them or assumed that the bishop or stake president would contact them. When appropriate, share with the family about the missionary's service and strengths. Consider downloading the free *Short Guide for Parents* on earlyRM.com for them to read through on their way to the airport.

Short Guide for Ward Councils

This guide is for ward councils but also a reference for all ward members. Like a convert, early RMs may struggle to find their place in the ward and need, as President Gordon B. Hinckley suggested, "a friend, a responsibility, and nurturing with 'the good word of God' (Moro. 6:4)." You have the wonderful opportunity to help these missionaries feel welcomed, needed, and loved.

If I could tell you one thing:

You do not need to know why a missionary came home. Simply welcome them home and express your love for them. Find ways to get them engaged in the ward again.

1. Make sure they have "a friend."

Every early RM needs a friend: someone who will not judge or ask personal questions but quietly give support and love during this time, especially as many of the missionary's peers may still be in the mission field. This friend may be someone their own age, someone who came home early from a mission in the past, or a person with lots of time to give (such as an elderly member of the ward). Consider the possibility of assigning a separate set of visiting teachers or home teachers (from the parents) to the missionary for more individual support.

2. Give them "a responsibility."

Transitioning home from 24/7 service on the mission is very difficult for most. Ward councils can discuss ways for an early RM to have a calling or a responsibility. A responsibility gives the missionary a sense of purpose and meaning and a hint of their mission life. A responsibility gives a missionary another reason to come to church. A responsibility often helps other members welcome them more. If health or unworthiness is an issue, think of creative ways to give this missionary an opportunity to serve.

3. Nurture them with "the good word of God."

Although not all early RMs will struggle with their testimonies when they return, many feel shaken and unsure of how to proceed. More than anything, these missionaries need "nurturing" with the gospel. They need faith-building environments to ask the questions they may be struggling with. They need opportunities to feel the Spirit. They need to be able to teach the doctrine. Pray to know how to carefully provide these opportunities to them. If you want an early RM to give a talk or share a mission story in a lesson or teach in mission prep, gently ask them *beforehand* if they would be comfortable doing so. Support them if they feel they are not ready or need more time to prepare.

4. Support the family of the early RM.

While most expect the early RM to struggle, sometimes the needs of the family around them are forgotten. Parents may be grieving for the loss of the mission too and may struggle just as much as (or more than) their child. They may to struggle to know how to parent an adult child during this time when a missionary may be extremely dependent on their emotional support, finances, and testimony. Siblings may not know why a missionary is home and may feel confused as to why everything is so different from the last time they saw their sibling at the airport. Supporting the family as you would through any trial and ensuring that the family has steady home teachers and visiting teachers is vital.

Acknowledgements

To each of the missionaries I interviewed and surveyed, this book would not have happened without you being willing to be vulnerable and open. Thank you for sharing your extremely personal stories, deepest fears, and lessons learned so that other early RMs may (we hope) have a better transition home than we did.

A special thanks to Ryan Freeman and his research team who donated a monster-sized file of early RM survey responses that got the ball rolling. And to each of the volunteer editors and reviewers who have helped my first book get off the ground, specifically Mindy Selu, Heather Low, Amy Whitcomb, Elizabeth Snyder, Marianne Kunzler, and Bishop Wilkinson.

And finally, to Brad Wilcox, Christopher Phillips, Doug Richens, Megan Rogers, Jan Pinborough, and LaRene Gaunt. Thank you for encouraging me to help members in need through the written word.

———

And now to give my thanks in ways only you will understand:

Sunshine Nestor - for singing "ne felj" and pointing out miracles
Heather Low - for much needed jokes no one would dare utter
Janae Andersen - for swine flu infested hugs and sensitivity
Hailey Barker - for morning dances and szeretet bombas

Dad - for strength, consistency, and testimony
Mom - for discernment and understanding
Micah - for bear hugs that fix *everything*
Abram - for texts and talks that keep me going
Hyram - for an indexing addiction and lots of I Love Lucy
Jonas - for awesome snuggles and that epic mid-faint foot catch

Liz Snyder - for six years of sistership
Ashley Millsap - chicken roommates forever!
Malia Mullenaux - for late night, *real* conversations
Fox Fam - for many a surprise "sleep-overs" and much needed hugs
JoMae Brenneke - for being the best online mission trainer ever
Aunt Joyce and Uncle Mike - for *constant* love and support

Mindy Selu - for a mad rush weekend of editing
Shayna Collier-Nelson - for your talent to create the perfect cover

As well as Dunaway, Edit, Szandi, Magdi, Egan, Vaterlaus, McRae, and Pickerd who reached out to me after the mission. And, of course, my MTC teachers: Snow, Sorenson, and Petty. Szeretlek benneteket!

Bibliography

Barlow, Britt. Skype Interview. 3 July 2015.

Bednar, David A. "Receiving, Recognizing, and Responding to the Promptings of the Holy Ghost." Ricks College Devotional. Idaho, Rexburg. 31 Aug. 1999. BYU Idaho.

Benedict, Jeff. The Mormon Way of Doing Business: Leadership and Success through Faith and Family. New York: Warner Business, 2007. Print.

Brown, Hugh B. "God Is the Gardener." BYU Devotional. Utah, Provo. 31 May 1968. BYU Speeches.

Cordon, Bonnie H. "Trust in the Lord and Lean Not." LDS General Conference. Utah, Salt Lake City. Apr. 2017. LDS.org.

Crockett, Chandler. Phone Interview. 29 Dec. 2015.

Dew, Sheri. "This is a Test. It is Only a Test." BYU Women's Conference. 1 May 1998.

Dickson, Courtney. Live Interview. 10 Aug. 2015.

Farnworth, Lindsay. Email Interview. 10 Nov. 2015.

Freeman, Ryan. Email Interview. 3 Aug. 2015.

Friedmann, Pascal. Skype Interview. 14 Aug. 2015.

Hansen, Christie. Email Interview. 13 Sep. 2015.

Hedelius, Marissa. Email Interview. 7 Aug. 2015.

Hinckley, Gordon B. "Rise to the Stature of the Divine within You." LDS General Conference. Utah, Salt Lake City. Oct. 1989. LDS.org.

Hobson, Alan, and Jamie Clarke. The Power of Passion: Achieve Your Own Everests. Calgary: Everest Effort, 1997. Print.

Holland, Jeffrey R. "An High Priest of Good Things to Come." LDS General Conference. Utah, Salt Lake City. Oct. 1999. LDS.org.

Holland, Jeffrey R. "Be Ye Therefore Perfect - Eventually." LDS General Conference. Utah, Salt Lake City. Oct. 2017. LDS.org.

Holland, Jeffrey R. "Lessons from Liberty Jail." BYU Devotional. Utah, Provo. 07 Sept. 2008. BYU Speeches.

Holland, Jeffrey R. "Lord, I Believe" LDS General Conference. Utah, Salt Lake City. Apr. 2013. LDS.org.

Holland, Jeffrey R. "The Best Is Yet to Be." Ensign. The Church of Jesus Christ of
    Latter-day Saints, Jan. 2010.
Ikahihifo, Shauna. "Repentance Is Real." Ensign. The Church of Jesus Christ of
    Latter-day Saints, Apr. 2015.
Jones, Chelsea. Skype Interview. 14 Aug. 2015.
Jones, Hunter. Live Interview. 20 Oct. 2015.
Lethco, Darcy. Live Interview. 24 July 2015.
Lindmeir, Kiana. Skype Interview. 15 Aug. 2015.
Monson, Thomas S. "The Will Within." LDS General Conference. Utah, Salt
    Lake City. Apr. 1987. LDS.org.
"Mountains to Climb." Mormon Channel, 20 Feb. 2015.
Olsen, Aaron. "When a Missionary Returns Early." Article. LDSLiving.com.
"Online Survey of Self-Reported RMs with In-Field Illness or Injury."
    SickRMs.com. Survey. Collected Oct. 2013 to Feb. 2014.
Rasband, Ronald A. "By Divine Design." LDS General Conference. Utah, Salt
    Lake City. Oct. 2017. LDS.org.
Rice, Micaela. Email Interview. 25 Aug. 2015.
Richards, Andriana. Email Interview. 27 Apr. 2015.
Stevenson, Madison. Email Interview. 12 Aug. 2015.
Tyler, Parker. Live Interview. 2016.
Uchtdorf, Dieter F. "You Can Do It Now!" LDS General Conference. Utah, Salt
    Lake City. Oct. 2013. LDS.org.
Van Heel, Amy. Email Interview. 8 Nov. 2015.
Westbrook, Megan. Facebook Messenger Interview. 13 Sep. 2015.
Wilcox, Brad. "His Grace Is Sufficient." BYU Devotional. Utah, Provo. 12 July
    2011. BYU Speeches.
Yarbro, Destiny. "Catching the Vision: All Missions Bring Souls to Christ."
    Ensign. Aug. 2015.
Yarbro, Destiny. "Mission Photo in Budapest." 2009.
Yarbro, Destiny. "The Lord Protects His Missionaries." Don't Stop Sargeant.
    Wordpress. 15 Apr. 2015.

Notes

Notes

Notes

Author Bio

Destiny Yarbro loves visiting the branches of the church throughout the world. In between trips, she enjoys being a social entrepreneur and creating resources to help members with specific life challenges, such as having a disability, being homebound, having a mental illness, being incarcerated, etc. She loves hiking, playing the piano, writing, and teaching.

www.DestinyYarbro.com
Facebook: facebook.com/destiny.yarbro
Instagram: @ldsnomad
Email: yarbro.destiny@gmail.com

Made in the USA
San Bernardino, CA
24 November 2017